SIX TEMPLES AT THEBES.

1896.

BY

W. M. FLINDERS PETRIE, D.C.L., LL.D., Ph.D.,

EDWARDS PROFESSOR OF EGYPTOLOGY, UNIVERSITY COLLEGE, LONDON;
VICE-PRESIDENT OF THE ROYAL ARCHÆOLOGICAL INSTITUTE, LONDON;
MEMBER OF THE IMPERIAL GERMAN ARCHÆOLOGICAL INSTITUTE;
CORRES. MEMBER SOCIETY OF ANTHROPOLOGY, BERLIN;
MEMBER OF THE SOCIETY OF NORTHERN ANTIQUARIES.

WITH A CHAPTER BY

WILHELM SPIEGELBERG, Ph.D.,
OF STRASSBURG UNIVERSITY.

Copyright © 2011 Read Books Ltd.
This book is copyright and may not be
reproduced or copied in any way without
the express permission of the publisher in writing

British Library Cataloguing-in-Publication Data
A catalogue record for this book is available from
the British Library

Flinders Petrie

William Matthew Flinders Petrie was born on 3rd July 1853 in Kent, England, son of William Petrie and Ann Flinders. The young Flinders Petrie was educated at home in a devout Christian household due to his father being a member of the Plymouth Brethren.

He showed an early interest in the field of archaeology and by his teenage years was surveying local Roman monuments near his family home. This enthusiasm resulted in a visit to Egypt in 1880 to study the great Pyramid at Giza, where his analyses were the first to apply observation and logic to investigate how the pyramids were constructed. His meticulous accuracy in measurement still provides a considerable amount of the basic data still used today in the study of the pyramid plateau.

His impressive scientific approach to the field earned him the position of professor at University College London. This recognition secured Filnders Petrie the funds he needed for excavation projects, and in 1884 he returned to Egypt to continue his work.

He would often have over 150 workmen on his digs but would choose to be the foreman of the operation himself. He was popular with his workers, and by reducing the pressure on them to make quick finds, they were able to toil more carefully and unearth small but significant artefacts that would otherwise have been lost or damaged.

Flinders Petrie continued to have many successes in Egypt and Palestine throughout his career, most notably, his discovery of the Mernepte stele, a stone tablet depicting scenes from ancient times. He also developed new excavation methods which revolutionised large scale digging operations. He went on to produce a wealth of publications on his subject, including *A Season in Egypt, 1887* (1888), *Koptos* (1896), *Methods & Aims in Archaeology* (1904), and many more. His excellent methodology and plethora of finds earned him a Knighthood for his services to archaeology in 1923.

In 1896, Flinders Petrie married Hilda Urlin, with whom he had two children, John and Ann. After his retirement, he and Hilda moved to Jerusalem where they lived at the British School of Archaeology. He remained there until his death in July 1942.

CONTENTS.

INTRODUCTION.

SECT.		PAGE
1.	The produce of excavations	1
2.	Site of the work	1
3.	The workmen	2
4.	A retrospect	2
5.	My fellow-workers	2

CHAPTER I.

THE CHAPEL OF UAZMES, ETC.

6.	Excavation in the chapel	3
7.	Works of the early XVIIIth dynasty	3

CHAPTER II.

THE TEMPLE OF AMENHOTEP II.

8.	History of the site	4
9.	Arrangement of temple	4
10.	Foundation deposits, etc.	5
11.	Stele of Duaui-er-neheh	5
12.	Jar of 26th year, and pottery	5
13.	Building by Amenhotep III	6
14.	Chapel of the white queen	6

CHAPTER III.

THE TEMPLE OF TAHUTMES IV.

15.	Condition of the site	7
16.	Forecourt of temple	7
17.	Burial of workmen	7

SECT.		PAGE
18.	Plan of the temple	8
19.	Sculptures found	9

CHAPTER IV.

THE WORK OF AMENHOTEP III.

20.	Destruction of his temple	9
21.	Avenue of jackals	9
22.	Statues	10
23.	Limestone stele	10
24.	Black granite stele	10

CHAPTER V.

THE TEMPLE OF MERENPTAH.

25.	Foundations	11
26.	Arrangement of temple	11
27.	The altars in temples	12
28.	Brick store chambers	12
29.	Black granite stele, and statues	13

CHAPTER VI.

THE TEMPLE OF TAUSERT.

30.	Site and plan	13
31.	Foundation deposits	14
32.	Description of plates XVI, XVII	14
33.	Relation of Tausert to Siptah	15

CHAPTER VII.

THE TEMPLE OF SIPTAH.

34.	Site and plan	16
35.	Foundation deposits	16

CHAPTER VIII.

LATER OBJECTS AND PLAN.

SECT.		PAGE
36.	Drawings	17
37.	Tomb of Khonsuardus	18
38.	Scarp behind Tausert	18
39.	Helmet and tools	18
40.	Description of iron tools	18
41.	Relations of temples	19

CHAPTER IX.

THE INSCRIPTIONS.

By Dr. W. Spiegelberg.

42.	Inscriptions of Pl. I	20
43.	„ „ II	21
44.	„ Pls. V, VIII	21
45.	„ Pl. IX	21
46.	Limestone stele of Amenhotep III, Pl. X	23
47.	Granite stele of Amenhotep III, Pls. XI, XII	23
48.	Granite stele of Merenptah, Pls. XIII, XIV	26
49.	Stele of Duaui-er-neheh, Pl. XV	28
50.	Wine jars, etc., Pls. XVI–XX	29
51.	Note on Israel stele	30

CHAPTER X.

SHELLS USED BY THE EGYPTIANS.

52.	List of shells	30

LIST OF PLATES.

Plate.		Page
1. Reliefs of XVIIIth dynasty		3, 4, 9, 20
2. Statuettes of XVIIIth dynasty		4, 5, 21
3. Foundation deposits and small objects, XVIIIth dynasty		5, 7, 9, 13, 21
4. Pottery from deposits, early XVIIIth dynasty		3, 4, 5
5. Pottery of Amenhotep II and III.		5, 21
6. Portraits of kings. (*Photograph*)		6, 9, 10, 13, 17, 22
7. Pottery of Tahutmes IV		8
8. Steles of XVIIIth–XXth dynasty		6, 9, 17, 18, 21
9. Inscriptions of XVIIIth dynasty, etc.		4, 6, 9, 21, 22
10. Limestone stele of Amenhotep III triumphing. (*Photograph*)		10, 23
11. Black granite stele of Amenhotep III. (*Photograph*)		10, 23
12. Inscription of same		23
13. Black granite stele of Merenptah. (*Photograph*)		13, 26
14. Inscription of same		26
15. Stele of Duaui-er-neheh. (*Photograph*)		5, 28
16. Deposit of Tausert, small objects.		14, 29
17. Deposit of Tausert and Siptah, pottery		14, 15, 16, 17
18. Deposit of Siptah, small objects		16, 29
19. Ostraka of Tausert and of Siptah		29
20. Ostraka from Amenhotep II to Merenptah		9, 29
21. Helmet, bowl, and tools. (*Photograph*)		18, 19
22. General plan of temples		7, 13, 19
23. Plan of temples of Amenhotep II and white queen		4
24. Plan of temple of Tahutmes IV.		7
25. Plan of temple of Merenptah		11
26. Plans of temples of Uazmes, Tausert, Siptah, and Khonsuardus		3, 13 16, 18

INTRODUCTION.

1. Repeatedly ransacked as the region of Thebes has been in all past times, there yet remain a few parts which have been little examined, if at all. The cemetery has been turned over and over by every plunderer, from the old Egyptian down to the Coptic dealer of last year; but the temple sites, from their wide extent and the paucity of small objects to be found in them, have been but little searched. It was accordingly on these temple sites that we spent our work in 1896; and though the results were less in some ways than I had hoped, yet in others they far exceeded what could have been expected.

On looking back over past years of work, the general result altogether is that out of any ten great results that are anticipated and worked for, only five will be successfully attained; but ten other results wholly unexpected will be found in the course of the work. Thus if on the one hand we only get half of what we expect, on the other hand our unimagined results are equal to all that we looked for. Another general conclusion is that following definite clues produces but a small proportion of the successes; much more than half of the discoveries proceed from making very extensive and thorough clearances, acres in extent, and yards deep to the very bottom, on ground which is likely to contain important material. While in cemeteries, only one tomb in ten repays the work; and it is the rare one tomb in a hundred that compensates for the ninety blanks and nine scanty results.

2. The region of the work was about half a mile long, and a furlong wide, along the desert edge of the western shore of Thebes. This ground reached from behind the Kom el Hettan to near the temple of Tahutmes III. When I went there in December, 1895, the temples already known in this ground were those of Tahutmes IV, and Ramessu II, and between them the chapel of Uazmes, discovered in 1887; while the ruins behind the Kom el Hettan were attributed to Amenhotep III. The result of my work was to fix the last-named ruin as the temple of Merenptah, and to discover the sites of the temples of Amenhotep II, Tausert, and Siptah; at the same time the sites of Tahutmes IV and of Uazmes were fully cleared and planned. Meanwhile Mr. Quibell cleared the Ramesseum and the great buildings around that, working for the Egyptian Research Account.

To excavate in this place, we settled in the brick galleries, which formed the store-chambers and barracks of Ramessu II around the Ramesseum. Most of these galleries or tunnels have fallen in during the slow decay of thirty centuries, but some of them are yet complete enough to give all the shelter that is needed in such a climate. We picked up loose bricks in the ruins, and built dry walls to divide the long space into rooms. Each gallery is about thirteen feet wide and high, and the remaining portions are, some of them, about eighty feet long. One shorter gallery served for my room and store for antiquities; the next, which was a long one, was divided up for Mr. and Miss Quibell, two spare rooms for some time occupied by Miss Pirie and Miss Paget while they were copying paintings, our dining-room and the kitchen; the next gallery contained about sixty workmen and boys, with very often half a dozen donkeys and an occasional camel; and another short gallery served for my best man Ali and his family, and the mother of another of the men. We thus formed a compact community in what was almost a fortification, as I had cleared out a deep trench around the dwellings so as to prevent any outsiders coming about the place or getting on our roof; while on the top of the brick arches of the galleries was a wide level space, which served for spreading things in the sun. Very soon we had to enclose a space in front of the galleries to hold our collections of pottery, pieces of sculpture, and stacks of ushabtis.

B

INTRODUCTION.

3. At first I brought up some of our best men from Koptos, and took on many of the Qurneh people for the work. But as soon as we began to find antiquities, it was evident that the previous engagements of these local workers to the various dealers of Thebes took precedence of their engagement to me. Thus, half or more of what they found was abstracted for their old friends, although I was paying them so well for things that I even bought back from dealers part of what had been taken, at the same rate that I paid the workmen. It was not a case of greater gain to them, but of obliging their dealer friends with stock for trade. This system was quickly defeated by dismissing all the local workers, excepting a few boys and negroes, and bringing in a far larger garrison from Koptos, while also drawing many from the villages around. Thus, for two months, we completely defeated the endless machinations of the Luxor and Qurneh dealers, and the petty terrorism which they tried to exercise. So long as I had Qurneh men, I heard within twenty-four hours of what was stolen, through reports sent to me from Luxor; so soon as I dismissed them, I never heard of anything else going astray, nor had my good and honest old friend Muhammed Mohassib at Luxor any knowledge of anything reaching there. So for the first time excavations at Thebes were carried on clear of the incessant pilfering and loss which had been hitherto supposed inevitable. Nothing short of a good garrison of trained workers from a distance, entrenched upon the work, kept in hand day and night with good *esprit de corps*, prohibited under pain of dismissal from going to the villages around, or from buying or borrowing anything from the neighbours, together with continual watchfulness and a free use of fire-arms at night— nothing short of this will suffice for excavations at Thebes. With this system we had the satisfaction of digging up scarabs and other good things a few inches below where the enraged Qurnawis had been walking all their lives, without their being able to touch a single piece. My man Ali Suefi was even more valuable than before, as he was not only proof against all the blandishments of the local rascals—the Abd er Rasuls and others—but harassed them in any attempt to get at the other workers, and saved us a large part of our results. Of course I put him on to all the best places, and he got about half of all the bakhshish of the season as his reward. When you have an honest man, make it worth his while to continue so.

4. The whole of my work in this season here described was, as in past years, carried on with the assistance of my constant friends, Mr. Jesse Haworth and Mr. Martyn Kennard. After nine years of this association a change has come, by my working for the Egypt Exploration Fund; but a change which leaves much regret in closing—at least for the present—the most cordial and pleasant relations which have cheered my work for so long a time. But for the ready help of these friends in providing for excavations, to whatever extent seemed required, it would have been impossible for us now to look back on the portraits of Hawara, which restored to us the Greco-Roman art of painting; the pyramids of Amenemhat III, and Usertesen II, the first that were shown to be of the XIIth dynasty; the towns of Kahun and Gurob, with the insight into the XIIth and XVIIIth dynasties that they gave us; the XIIth dynasty papyri, and the Ptolemaic papyri; the clearing of Medum, which fixed the pottery and the hieroglyphs of the beginning of history; the painting and other arts of the naturalistic age of Tell el Amarna; the prehistoric works of Koptos; the opening of an entirely new position by the history of the New Race at Naqada; and lastly, the Theban temples and the great stele naming the Israelite War. All of these results are due to the public spirit of the two friends who have been ever ready to let me draw on their purses for such work. My best thanks, and those of the public are due to them, for thus assisting in filling up our knowledge of ancient Egypt. How much this means we may feel by just trying to imagine what our views would now be without this insight, at almost every age, into the civilization and works of that country.

5. In the preparation of this volume, Dr. Spiegelberg has rendered much assistance in undertaking the editing of the inscriptions. While I was excavating, he was staying at Thebes for studying the graffiti of the Ramesside age, and as his researches lay specially in that period, it seemed most fitting that he should proceed to work over the ostraka and other hieratic inscriptions that I found. Subsequently the great prize of the Israel inscription—one of the longest and most complete that is known—was brought to light; and Dr. Spiegelberg copied it, worked over my squeeze of it, and published the text in the "Zeitschrift." His contribution to the present volume will show how fully he has laboured at the material which we collected, first in Egypt, and afterwards in England and Germany. The drawings here given are my own;

and for the photographs reproduced, I have to thank Mr. Frank Haes for those taken in England, and Brugsch Bey for those of the steles kept at the Ghizeh Museum. Continually I have had the benefit of Mr. Quibell's help, both in finishing my affairs in Egypt, and in working over the materials brought away. So this year, as before, many friends make short work.

I should add that although the general direction of these temples is facing south-east, yet for convenience they are assumed to face east, in accord with the general north to south direction of the Nile Valley, and all directions are described in accord with the temples facing east and backing west. It will be noticed that the plans of buildings are all to a uniform scale, so that they can be compared together.

CHAPTER I.

THE CHAPEL OF UAZMES, AND THE EARLY XVIIITH DYNASTY.

6. This chapel or small temple lies immediately beyond the road south of the Ramesseum. It was discovered and cleared out by M. Daressy in 1887; and a plan of it was published as PL. IV in "Le Musée Égyptien," of which only "Tom. I, Liv. I, Fasc. I" ever appeared, so that the promised text which was to come in Fascicule II has not been published. As this exploration bared the whole site it might seem needless to say more about it; but a small further excavation gave important results.

The present state of the chapel is given in PL. XXVI, where the solid black shows the remaining brick walls, the open outlines at the doorways show the stonework, and the open outline of walls show what has disappeared since the uncovering in 1887. Several details shown on the earlier plan cannot now be traced out; but in one respect—the skew of the south side of the forecourt—the later plan is the more accurate. This skew was specially noticed as affecting the question of estimating the mean axis of the building.

Some few matters yet waited to be examined. At A the sandstone sill of the entrance pylon remains in place. The two lines crossing it show where the sides of the doorway stood. On tunnelling beneath it there was found a blue glazed ring of Amenhotep III of a fine colour (PL. III, 26). From the position it does not seem at all likely that this can have been introduced after the building, and hence we must attribute a restoration of this chapel to Amenhotep III. What his object was in thus working here we may guess when we see that he took the temple of Amenhotep II, and largely altered it for a temple in honour of the Princess Sitamen, daughter of Amenhotep III. Probably therefore he made a similar re-appropriation of this chapel for some divinity or for some other princess of his family. At B, at the head of the low steps leading to the court, at 28 inches deep, upon the gravel, were seventeen little dumps of blue glazed pottery, about $\frac{1}{4}$ inch across. At C was found a fine green glazed scarab of Amenhotep II (PL. III, 25) apparently beneath the brickwork of the door sill. And at D were three more blue glazed dumps and a flower, rather like that of Merenptah's foundations (PL. III, 30). Along the west side of the building is a thick bed of rubbish and pottery, and on digging through part of that a piece of a blue glazed bowl was found (PL. III, 27) which is broken at a tantalising point after the title of the "Divine wife of Amen," so that the name is just lost. The colour and drawing of this piece are like works of Amenhotep III, but very different to the earlier style of Hatshepsut. So this again shows that the activities at this place belong to the later date.

On looking at the sculptures found here in 1887, and published in PLS. I, II, III, V, VI, of "Le Musée Égyptien," about half of them belong to the earlier age, down to Tahutmes III (PLS. I, II, V A, VI B, D); while others are of the later part of the XVIII dynasty (III, VI C) and probably early XIX dynasty (V B, C; VI A). The official of the cemetery Pa-shed who adores Uazmes on the stele of PL. III is very probably the same as the cemetery official Pa-shed of the Belmore altar No. 8, and the tablets 261, 262, 264, 282, 341 of the British Museum. (The numbers here given are those in the Synopsis of 1850, the only available list of that Museum). It seems therefore that this chapel was in use for the adoration of Uazmes, and perhaps of other persons, down to the XIXth dynasty; and that it was largely restored under Amenhotep III.

7. Some other remains of the early part of the XVIIIth dynasty were found in various sites: we here notice them in the order of the drawings.

In the temple of Tahutmes IV blocks of earlier sculpture had been freely used up: some of these appear to have been from tombs, as they bear figures of servants (PL. I, 1, 2). The date is shown by the cartouche of Tahutmes I and the name Aa-kheper-ka-ra-senb. These slabs are of coarse brown sandstone painted in body colour, without any sculpturing.

A tablet (PL. I, 3) of limestone shows a woman named Bakt, making a meat offering and a drink offering to the cow of Hahtor, for the benefit of her husband, the engraver of Amen, named Amenemhat. The three hollows at the top are apparently for two ears, and perhaps the sign of a hide; it seems as if some inlaid objects had been inserted, of glass or metal.

A portion of an altar (PL. I, 4) of sandstone dedicated by a chief priest of Tahutmes III named Ra, was found in the temple ruins of Amenhotep II. This priest was the husband of the nurse of Amenhotep II, and his tomb is one of the finest in Qurneh, published partly in Lepsius "Denkmaler" III, 62, and Prisse "Art," where the glass and stone vases are figured.

A large wooden ushabti (PL. II, 1) was found in a high heap of ashes upon the top of the brick galleries behind the Ramesseum: how it can have come into such a position cannot be traced. It belonged to the tomb of the great viceroy of the Sudan under Tahutmes III, named Nehi; he built the temple in the island of Sai, and carved the S. grotto of Ibrim. The work of this ushabti shows the taste of that time in the slender, delicately carved, and finely formed hieroglyphs.

A limestone Osiride figure (PL. II, 2) of Tahutmes I was found in the ruins of the temple of Amenhotep II; the work however seems to belong to the time of the earlier king, and it seems as if it might well have been brought from his tomb, and be an early type of royal ushabti.

Behind the temenos of the temple of Merenptah, we found at the base of the wall a patch of sand with small vases (PL. IV, 1–8) of rough pottery; and it appears that these belonged to the foundation deposit of some earlier building, which was cleared away by Merenptah. These seem on the whole to be rather earlier in type than the vases of Amenhotep II, figured next below them: but no positive date can be assigned to them.

On clearing a building in the outer court of Tahutmes IV, a part of an earlier stele was found used up in the threshold (PL. IX, 1). It represents a man named Min-mes, making offerings to his father Athu-usir; and from the work it is probably of about the reign of Tahutmes III.

These comprise all the remains earlier than Amenhotep II which were found in the course of the excavations. The later remains we shall notice in dealing with the temples of their respective periods in the following chapters.

CHAPTER II.

THE TEMPLE OF AMENHOTEP II.

8. To the north of the Ramesseum was a space of ground covered with chips of stone, and with a few brick walls showing upon it. When examined this proved to be a confused mass of structures of four different ages. First of all there had been some brick buildings, askew to the later plan; these had traces of colour on them, and were probably chapels of some tombs. A piece of this wall is shown on the north side of the plan, PL. XXIII, at A. The next building was the temple of Amenhotep II; and the occurrence of his name here cannot be due merely to his materials being brought from some other site at a later date, as five foundation deposits of his were found quite undisturbed in the rock.

Next Amenhotep III largely altered this temple. Sculptured blocks of Amenhotep II are found re-used, buried in the foundations of the colonnade of the portico; this re-use was before Amenhotep IV, as the name of Amen is not erased upon them, while it is erased on all the sculptures left above ground. Thus we are limited to Tahutmes IV or Amenhotep III in our ascription of the rebuilding; and it is fixed to the latter king by the many pieces of glazed pottery tubes, from some furniture, bearing his name. Probably to this time, or a little later, belong the many pieces of limestone with trial sculptures of some students, who seem to have used the temple as a school.

The last use of this site was for tombs of about the XXIInd dynasty. The walls of these are shown by mottled black and white on the plan. Within the enclosures were three tomb pits, marked here by diagonal lines. So much for the history of the site.

9. Turning now to the details of the temple of Amenhotep II, the only parts that we can be certain are original are the bases of the columns (as the deposits are undisturbed beneath them), and the stone foundations of walls which are built like the bases. The court was not so large as that of Tahutmes IV, and had only a single line of columns around it, the whole being about 140 feet wide, and 120 feet long.

The position of the back wall is shown by the great door sill B. At C was the grey granite statue of Amenhotep II, swathed in osiride manner, and holding the crook and flail—a type unusual in a seated statue such as this. The head was broken off, and could not be found anywhere in the whole site. From the position it seems that the statue was one of a pair on either side of the entrance to the temple beyond the court. Such was also the position of the statues of Ramessu and of Merenptah in their temples. Beyond this there are fragments of foundations left, but not enough to indicate a plan. The proportion of the front court to the length of the site behind it is more like that of Tahutmes IV than like the longer temples of the XIXth dynasty.

10. The foundation deposits were of two classes. There were the usual pits in the rock, containing rough alabaster vases, inscribed in ink with the cartouche (PL. III, 5), corn grinders (III, 1) of sandstone, oval pieces of alabaster (III, 2, 3, 4), copper models of adzes (III, 6), chisels (III, 8, 9), axes (7), and knives (10); with these were a large quantity of rough pottery vases (IV, 9–29). These deposits are marked D in the plan, and it is remarkable how they are scattered about the site, and not in the usual positions; the three under the line of column bases are strangely close together. The other class of deposits were the small limestone tablets with the cartouches (III, 11, 12); these were found in pairs, face to face, on the ground surface under the ruins.

Of miscellaneous objects found here were some bronze rosettes, gilt, and pierced with holes for sewing on to a garment (III, 17). Many pieces of finely-carved statuettes of wood were scattered about, and a headless kneeling figure of alabaster (II, 3), probably of Amenhotep II, as other figures in this attitude are known of him at Paris, Berlin, and Turin, and are drawn in a tomb at Qurneh. The portion of an osiride statuette of Tahutmes I (II, 2) is most unexpected in such a position; it seems more likely to have come from his temple or tomb.

11. The broken altar of Ra, high priest of Tahutmes III (I, 4), was found in the ruins (see " History " II, 162, 163), as also the large unfinished stele of Duaui-er-neheh, reproduced in photograph PL. XV. This man cannot be the same as Duaui-neheh of Qurneh, tomb 22 (in *Champollion, Notices*, I, 515, 844), whose mother was Tarounet ("the virgin"), as this man's mother was Mesut. But as both men have the same hereditary titles, and each has a brother, a *uab* priest, named Neb-mes, it seems likely that this man was grandson of the owner of the Qurneh tomb, son he cannot be, as his father was Benaa. We might therefore restore the family thus:—

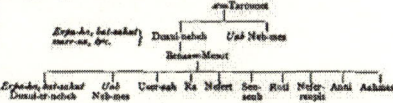

This would agree well in date. The Qurneh tomb bears the names of Hatshepsut and Tahutmes III, about 1500 or 1490 B.C.; and this tablet was left unfinished and used in the building of Amenhotep II, about 1440 B.C., thus leaving 50 or 60 years between the two for the two generations that elapsed. The main interest of the stele is its unfinished condition. The position of all the figures and signs has been first sketched in red; then the final outlines have been drawn in delicate black line over all the figures and the inscription at the top, the names of the brothers and the first line of lower inscription being in solid black. Lastly a beginning of cutting has been made between the seated figures, just to show which part was to be sunk. The mode of writing the hieroglyphs is instructive, as a lesson in such writing, apart from hieratic forms. The exact formation of the strokes has been carefully copied and published by Miss Murray, in 'Proc. Soc. Bib. Arch.,' xix. 77. The discussion of the inscription is given in Dr. Spiegelberg's chapter here. The stele is now at University College, London.

12. Beside the pottery in the foundation deposits (IV 9–29), there were also found some jars lying in the ruins. One of these is of great value historically (V, 3), as it bears the name of Amenhotep II (V, 5), and a date of the twenty-sixth year (V, 6), with the name of the vine-dresser, Panehsi 'the negro,' who stored the wine. Hitherto no date of this king above the fifth year had been known, and the assignment of 25 years 10 months to this reign by Manetho was generally discredited. The latest writer, Maspero, asserts that the "reign was a short one, lasting ten years at most," ("Struggle of the Nations," 292). Yet from the generations in the royal genealogies, and the finishing of the Lateran obelisk after 35 years of abandonment, it seemed that Manetho's period must be correct (" History " ii. 153). Now there is absolute evidence for the whole length of reign named by Manetho, in this date of the 26th year, and we have a wholesome warning against rejecting his statements, except under the strongest pressure. Some other jars

were also found, the style of which agrees well with what we know of this period otherwise (V, 1, 2, 4). In the space to the north of the line of approach, close to the east of the portico, was an extensive levelling up of the ground with broken pottery. Among this pottery were many painted pieces, of which some are shown on PL. V, 7–12. The shading on these is upright for red, and horizontal for blue. The date of this filling up of the ground is not certain, for though it would seem probable that Amenhotep II would have required to level the ground, yet the bases of the columns here were all built by Amenhotep III from the ground upward for four courses. Hence it would be more likely that the material piled against the retaining wall of these foundations would also belong to the later king. The presence of much blue colouring on the pottery is in accord with this, for—so far as is yet known—this use of blue was introduced by Amenhotep III. A curious kind of pottery, not known otherwise, is incised with lines and spots, coloured white in alternate sections, and dabbed with white on the brown clay (III, 13).

13. The work of Amenhotep III on this site appears to have been an extensive remodelling. The whole of the portico was entirely built by him, as the foundation piers of the columns consist of pieces of sculpture of Amenhotep II, including a long lintel of sandstone broken in two. The sculptures in the temple were also due to him, for among the fragments is a relief of a princess, whose cartouche ends in *si* (VI. 6), which cannot be any known person but Sitamen, daughter of Amenhotep III. Another block bore the figures of a row of Libyans, and the work appears much more like that of the IIIrd than of the IInd Amenhotep. Many glazed tubes of pottery were found (III, 14, 15, 16, 18, 19, 20), coloured light blue, dark violet, and yellow, with inlays of dark blue and light green. These all bear the name of Amenhotep III, and refer to the festivals in which they were probably dedicated as part of some furniture. A beautiful bust from a small group in limestone, which was found here, appears from the hair to belong also to this age. A kneeling figure in grey syenite bears a tablet with adoration by a royal scribe, Sesh (VIII, 4), but as the head is lost, the reign cannot be assigned. In this region was also found a seal carved in pottery under Akhenaten, with the inscription "Aten temple" (III, 24).

The last use of this site was for a tomb chapel of about the XXIIIrd dynasty. The walls are shown in mottled black and white, and three tomb pits marked by diagonal lines. These pits were cleared out, but contained only very poor beads, and a bronze statue of a queen about eight inches high; this figure is apparently nude, with a circular crown, a short close wig (like the statue of Takushet in Athens), and wide flat sandals. Other figures of the same class are known. Some work was done here in Greek times, as a vase of Saitic period was found by the wall of this chapel, and with it an iron chisel and adze.

14. Behind the temple of Amenhotep II, toward the Ramesseum, stood another funerary chapel, which is shown on the plan PL. XXIII. The only object found in it is a bust of a queen in hard white limestone (VI, 2, 3), and hence this is called the White Queen's chapel. Unfortunately the name is lost, and only some priestly titles remain on the back of the bust (IX, 2). The date is quite unfixed; there is no very close parallel to the work, and only general considerations are available. Some points would lead to an early period, the locality just behind the temple of Amenhotep II and III, the hard white limestone just like that used by Amenhotep III, and the rosette on the breast, which is like that on the statue of Tua, wife of Sety I, in the Villa Verospi (Monumenti Inediti dall' Instituto, ii, 40). Dr. Spiegelberg remarks that he would place it to the XIXth dynasty, and calls attention to the wrinkle in the neck, which, so far as he has observed, is a peculiarity of the artist of the time of Sety I, and Ramessu II.

The double uraeus on the head is not decisive, as it occurs on Queen Tyi at Soleb, and on a later statue (of XXV dyn. ?) at Berlin; while a triple uraeus is on the head of Amenardus. The ear stud belongs equally to the XVIIIth and XXVth dynasties. But other points indicate a later date, of about the XXVth or XXVIth dynasties. The mention of Sais on the back would point to the XXVIth dynasty; though concentration of so many priesthoods into the queen's hands points also to the priestly character of the high priestesses of Amen. And the elaborate treatment of the hair seems quite as late as the XXVIth dynasty, and almost more like Ptolemaic work. On the whole I should be inclined to see in this one of the queens of the XXVIth dynasty, who held Thebes as being a ruler of the sacerdotal line.

The bust was found lying in the northern long chamber; it is now in the Cairo Museum. A few small fragments of coloured stucco were also found, but nothing distinct as to date; one piece reads,

"*kan mes suten hemt*." If this should be read as
". . . . ka . n born of the royal wife," there is only
one known person to whom it could refer, namely,
Psamtek III. Ra . ankh . ka . n born of the royal
wife Tentkheta. The difficulty in this, however, is
that there is no determination after the . . . . ka . n,
and, moreover, this being the throne name of Psamtek,
it could only occur after he was king, and yet the
. . . ka . n . is not in a cartouche. It more likely
refers then to some unknown prince, if it is a personal
name at all. The whole chapel is much denuded.
Of the north wall hardly anything remains above the
floor, and it is only visible as being above the ground
outside of it. The central chamber is about three or
four feet high. But the back wall is entirely gone,
and is here only restored at a guess.

CHAPTER III.

THE TEMPLE OF TAHUTMES IV.

15. The site of this temple was on a slight spur of
the desert edge next south of the chapel of Uazmes
and the Ramesseum (see PL. XXII). When we
began work there was an area of about two hundred
feet across, strewn with chips of sandstone and dust,
while east of it, lower down at the edge of the
cultivated land, were the worn down bases of
brick walls and pylons. The site has been identified
by Lepsius as belonging to Tahutmes IV., from the
cartouches stamped on the bricks, and the pylons are
marked on the map in the Denkmaler. But no attempt
to clear the temple site had yet been undertaken.

On PL. XXIV will be seen the plan of all the
existing remains. In some parts the sandstone
foundations of the walls and bases of the columns
were still in place. In far the larger part of the
building only the hollows in the rock cut for laying
the foundations could be traced; or, still worse, only
the hollow left by abstracting the stone from its bed
in the midst of clean rubble-filling, the hollow being
filled with stray rubbish. In these parts then it was
needful to notice the difference between old rubble
and later rubbish as the work went on. A few pieces
of original outer surface were left; as the granite
door sill of the peristyle court, marked G, two patches
of pavement in the inner part, marked P, and one
block of wall base with faces to it at the S.E. corner
of the court, marked B. The brick walling could be
traced around most of the site, though entirely
removed and denuded at the S.E. corner and along
the N. side.

16. Beginning with the entrance (see PL. XXIV),
at the east face there are parts of two massive
pylons, about 28 feet thick, which in a rounded state
are still about 10 feet high. The outer corners of the
terraces in front are almost entirely gone, but the bricks
can still be seen in the ground of the present road,
which runs just inside the outer pylons. Near the
north-west corner of the temenos are some brick buildings which are probably of Tahutmes IV, or Amenhotep III, judging by the pottery found in them.

Beyond this the rock is cut away in two hollows, one
on either side of the axis, so as to make a level court,
bounded by a rock face on the western side. The
axial roadway was dressed in a slope which ran up to
the top of the court and so led to the next terrace;
the arrangement being much like that of Deir el
Bahri. On the next terrace was a lesser pylon of
brickwork, about 68 feet (40 cubits) wide on either
side, and 18 feet thick. Behind this was another
court, levelled by being partly cut into the rock, so
that it was bounded on the west by a rock face, the
breadth of the latter of which is marked and shaded
with vertical shade lines. The rock on this western
side was faced over with a brick wall, and a stone
facing in front of that on the southern half. This
stone face is in line with the brick face of the northern
half, which therefore seems not to have any stone
face; if so, it was probably finished off last of all, and
time saved by putting only brickwork on the north,
to match the stone face on the south.

At the north end of this court the ground is higher,
and is occupied with a group of buildings, which were
divided into two parts, one of five rooms and a stairway, the other of eight rooms. The only object found
here was a rudely-cut stamp of limestone for sealing
wine jars (PL. III, 23).

17. In the south-west chamber of this building the
floor was found to rest upon made earth, and not on
the rock. On digging down here a rock scarp was
found facing the east, the slope of it being marked on
the plan by vertical shade lines. Below this scarp an
entrance was found, leading into a passage running
west; at the end of this passage a doorway admits to
a chamber cut in the rock, in which is a pit descending
to a lower level, and giving access to another passage
running east, with a tomb-chamber at the end of it.
The upper level passage and chamber are marked
on the plan with broken lines, the lower level passage
and chamber with dotted lines.

It is evident that this was a tomb considerably older than the temple; for when we opened it there was no trace of the original interment, but the upper passage and chamber was closely filled with at least two layers of bodies, over eighty being packed into it. And there was nothing in the lower passage and chamber. These bodies were scarcely to be called mummies, as they seemed to have been buried in wrappings without any attempt at preserving the flesh by resin, oil, or salts. Hence there was only a confused mass of bones amid a deep soft heap of brown dust. This burial-place cannot have been used later than the building of these chambers belonging to the temple, as the entrance was deeply covered with rubbish-filling to level the ground, and the walls rested on the rubbish. At the same time we cannot suppose such a common burial-ground to have been standing open for long before it was closed up for the temple building, as the bodies were quite undisturbed. Hence it seems probable that this was an older and plundered tomb, used as a common burying-place—perhaps for the workmen—during the reign of Tahutmes IV, or possibly Amenhotep II.

The only things found here with the bodies were plain vases of pottery. These were all collected, and the forms are shown on Pl. VII. The types are coarser and worse than some known to belong to Tahutmes III; compare Nos. 4, 8, 12, 13, and 18 with those from the Maket tomb at Kahun, in "Illahun" Pl. XXVII, Nos. 47, 34, 42, 40, and 49. There is also a type, No. 12, almost exactly like that found in the temple of Amenhotep II (Pl V, 1). All of the skulls from this tomb were brought to England, and some of the bones. There is a great diversity in the forms of the skulls, some being remarkably round, and others long. Had I realised their variation at first, I would have preserved the whole skeletons along with each; but presuming that they would be much of one type, being all of one place and date, I did not think it needful to do more than sample the skeletons. This great diversity suggests that these people were not natives of Thebes, but were probably foreign captives employed in the public works, and collected from all over Syria.

18. Passing now up the main axis, from the second court we reach a second terrace on which stood the portico of the temple. This must have been a fine structure, being 100 cubits wide (172 ft.), and having a double colonnade of fourteen columns. The width is the same as the temple of Sety I at Qurneh, but the columns were more slender and closer, being fourteen in place of ten. On the other hand, the depth of the double colonnade must have given an effect more like that of Deir el Baheri, where also the spacing of the columns is the same as here, though twenty or twenty-two are used in the front of that sumptuous temple as against fourteen here. Of these columns portions of only six basements remain, and mere hollows indicate the places of most of the others, though of nine of them no evidence was found and they are only shown by dotted outlines.

The great gate to the peristyle court of this temple had a threshold of red granite (marked G on the plan), of which the main part still remains. The square outline at the south end of it is the position of the jamb which can still be traced. At the south end of this front wall one stone yet remains above the foundation level, showing the dressed faces.

The peristyle court is unique in having a triple colonnade along the back and both sides. As only three out of eight columns have left any traces of foundation in the first two rows, it might seem not impossible that this might have been a hypostyle hall, of which all the central part had left no trace. But the northern half is so far complete in its evidences, not only the foundation, but the actual circular bases remaining, that we can hardly suppose it to have continued southward without leaving some sign either of stone or of rock cutting. It seems then that this is a unique piece of architecture in having a triple colonnade, and is also unusual in the number of columns. Here there are 14 × 9; the double colonnade of Luxor is 12 × 12, of the Ramesseum 8 × 10, and of Khonsu 6 × 6; while the great hall of Karnak (which is hypostyle), has the same number of columns as here, with a central avenue of larger ones in addition. There appears to have been a doorway on the south side with a porch over it, judging from the foundations. This is analogous to the doorway south of the forecourts of the temples of Ramessu II, Merenptah, and Ramessu III; it is probable therefore that it had a fixed ceremonial purpose, as it is repeated in four temples.

Of the shrine and back of the temple very little can be determined. There was a second columnar space, probably a shallow hall of six columns wide, and two or perhaps three deep. At each side of this there must have been a narrow chamber or passage: and behind this a row of small chambers, of which some foundations remain at the south-west. The ground along the south slopes is deeper to the west, so that the south-west corner is very low, lying in a small ravine that slopes across that corner of the temenos. Hence the foundations needed to be built to a considerable height; and to retain the chip filling around them brick walls were placed between the stone foundations, of which three are marked in solid black on the plan.

The temenos wall is cut across in the middle of the south side by a small ravine, so that the east end is north of the ravine and the west end and south-west corner is south of the ravine, isolated thus from the temple. The south-west corner is well preserved to a considerable depth, being buried in a deep bed of chips which formed the artificial levelling up of the ground at this part.

19. The sculptures found in the temple were but very few considering how much must have existed here. A slab of sandstone with a figure of Amen-Min in relief and painted, was found in the back part of the temple, and several coloured fragments which showed how the shrine had been decorated. Several large statues of Tahutmes IV were carved in limestone and painted; of these a few fragments were found, mostly ears. The lower part of one face is of value as a portrait (PL. VI, 4), and agrees closely with a relief of the king found also in this temple (PL. VI, 5).

A few tablets remained here. One mentioning a campaign to Ethiopia (PL. I. 8); another naming a fort in Syria called after the king (PL. I, 7). A fragment of a very rudely carved tablet may have been made by some Syrian workman; it represented Tahutmes IV adoring the goddess Asit, riding on horseback, armed with spear and shield as usual (PL. VIII, 1).

Within the temple area were found a plummet of green quartzose stone (PL. III, 21); and a part of a sistrum in blue glazed pottery (PL. III, 22).

Some rough hieratic quarrymarks were noted on the blocks of the foundation, of which three examples are given on PL. IX, 11-13. Nos. 11 and 12 mark the stones as for the building of the temple in the southern capital for his majesty; and No. 13 has the words "good years," which may be the personal name of a workman. On a piece of a large vase, found in the north-east buildings, were figured a pair of sandals and a bronze razor (PL. XX, 4); it seems not improbable that this was the price by barter of the jar of wine or oil on which they are marked. Two other pieces of hieratic inscriptions (PL. XX, 6, 7), are described by Dr. Spiegelberg.

CHAPTER IV.

THE WORK OF AMENHOTEP III.

20. On applying for permission to excavate at Thebes, M. de Morgan informed me that he reserved the site of the great funerary temple of Amenhotep III for his own work. The site of it is now largely under the high Nile level, as the water rises fourteen feet above the bases of the great colossi, and has deposited Nile mud to a height of eight feet above the bases. Hence the ground is now mainly cultivated, and expropriation of the cultivators is needful before working on the temple. The required ground had been already bought for the Government, as I was informed, and that site was, therefore, reserved. It happened, however, that, as I was allowed to work upon the desert the temple behind it, which I found to have been built by Merenptah, I there discovered a large amount of sculpture which had belonged to the temple of Amenhotep III, as that had been plundered for material by Merenptah. Hence, though I did not touch the great temple of Amenhotep III, I found what are very probably the most valuable remains of it. These are noticed here in the order in which they would have stood in the temple. I also found that Amenhotep III had largely re-arranged the temple built by Amenhotep II, in order to provide for the worship of his daughter Sitamen.

21. Many portions of gigantic couchant jackals were found, carved in soft sandstone. They had been split up into slices along the horizontal bedding of the stone, and laid in the foundations of Merenptah. The most complete that I measured was, from the tail, 52 inches to the toes of the hind foot, 92 to the elbow of the fore leg, 102 to the chest, and 114 to the broken stump of the paw: according to this the whole figure would have been about 135 inches long, and have needed, therefore, a base at least 11½ feet long. The width across the hind paws is 43 inches, and 45 at the fore legs. These jackals were couched upon bases of sandstone, having a torus and cavetto moulding round the top, a line of inscription below that, and a border of *dad* and *thet* girdle-tie alternately beneath the inscription. The lines of inscription are copied in PL. IX, 3 to 9. On the front end of these bases was some projecting mass; and as pieces of statues of Amenhotep III (see PL. VI, 9) of the same work and material are constantly found associated with these pieces, it seems most likely that the statues stood backing against the pedestals of the jackals.

c

The pedestals are 16 inches wide on either side of the statue, and allowing about 14 inches more for the width of the statue, the whole would be about 46 inches wide, or just suited for the jackals, which are 43 and 45 inches across the base.

Hence we may restore the avenue of approach to the temple of Amenhotep as being between the two lines of statues of the king in Osiride form, with *ankh* in each hand; the statues backed against high pedestals about 4 feet wide and 11½ feet long; upon which lay gigantic couchant jackals, the emblem of Anubis, under whose protection the dead king was placed. Upon the pedestals were also figures of a young priest wearing the panther's skin, who is stated to be the king's son, and probably is, therefore, Amenhotep IV—Akhenaten—in his boyhood.

22. Besides these jackals there were also limestone sphinxes, with the royal head. These were not so large, the bases being 65 × 19 inches. The head is not detailed, but merely blocked out and probably intended to be coloured (see PL. VI, 7). But the portraiture shows closely the same expression as in other heads of the king. Two of these sphinxes were dropped into a hole on their sides, head to tail, back to back, beneath one of the pillars. The limestone had somewhat swelled and cracked, so that the head of the perfect sphinx was loose, and I removed it therefore, leaving behind the body, and the other headless half.

Of statues, a face in black granite (see PL. VI, 8) was found, without any other parts of the figure. It is clearly a very careful piece of work, and probably one of the best portraits of the king, being in such a laboriously wrought material. It accords very closely with the expression of the other heads here, and the portraits elsewhere.

A body of a statue in limestone, painted about life size, was found in the southern foundations of the first court of Merenptah. On the western side of that court, in the foundations, are fragments of a colossal group of the king and a god, carved in very hard white crystalline limestone with exquisite finish; a fragment of the hieroglyphs is copied in PL. I, 5. On the northern side of the second court, in the foundations, is a head of a colossal statue in the same limestone, 50 inches through and 48 inches high. This would imply that it was 24 feet high, if a seated figure. Another head of the same limestone, near that, belonged to a sphinx; it is 60 inches from the chin to the back, which would imply a length of 21 feet. The head of a jackal in limestone, also near there, is 62 inches long. All these colossal heads of the king are battered and broken so much that they are not worth removal: but they, at least, show us how magnificent was the sculpture in material, execution, and size, which adorned the temple. Several blocks of limestone from the Amenhotep temple were used up; in particular, an enormous one in the N.W. corner of the first court of Merenptah lies face down. We tunnelled beneath it, and found a fine and perfectly preserved scene of offering, the carving of which retains its colouring intact.

23. Of the portable works of Amenhotep, two of special interest were found. The foundation of one column of Merenptah was formed of the two pieces of the limestone stele of PL. X, laid face down on the sand bed. The upper part of the stele shows Amenhotep making offerings to Amen: on the one side presenting Maat, the goddess of truth, on the other side presenting wine. The figures and names of Amen had been entirely erased from the stele, doubtless by Akhenaten, and have been re-sculptured on the erased surface by Sety I, who adds a line, saying: "Monumental restoration made by the son of the sun Mer-en-ptah Sety for his father Amen." Below this are two scenes: on the right hand the king in his chariot driving over the Negroes, on the left hand the king driving over the Syrians. Probably the stele was placed with its face westwards, so that the people of the north and the south looked to their respective sides; just as in the pylons of Tahutmes III and of Taharqa the northern people are north of the axis, and the southerners are to the south. At the base we read of the subjugation of all peoples, of Naharaina, and Kush, the miserable Reten, and the Upper Retenu under the feet of this good god, like the sun, for ever. The large size of this tablet, 6 feet high and 3½ feet wide, and the very delicate and finished style of its sculpture, makes it one of the finest works of this age.

24. The other stele is shown on plates XI, XII. It is a block of dark grey syenite, infiltrated with quartz veins: it is 10 feet 3 inches high, 5 feet 4 inches wide, and 13 inches thick; the condition is perfect with the exception of a small chip on one edge. The colouring is complete in the scene of Merenptah on the back of it; and some of the yellow colour remains in the scene of Amenhotep III.

The inscription and scene of Amenhotep III. has been largely erased by Akhenaten; the figures of Amen were removed, and all the inscription down to within a few lines of the bottom. The original face is still left at the bottom, along the edges, and around the figures of Amenhotep III; and these parts can be distinguished by the difference of reflection in the photograph. This erasure had not been complete enough to prevent the inscription being traceable, for the re-engraving of it under Sety I. had followed exactly the old lines, as is proved by a deeper bit of erasure occurring where the name of Amen comes in the re-engraving. And had it been re-engraved from a written copy preserved in the archives, there would not be certain mistakes in the text of one sign in place of another like it. Hence we conclude that Akhenaten had erased the inscription lightly, and only destroyed completely the names and figures of Amen.

After this, Sety I restored the whole inscription and figures, as he had done on the limestone tablet noticed above. He recorded his restoration in a column of deeply-cut signs, "Monumental restoration made by the king Maat-men-ra for his father Amen-Ra, king of all the gods." The translation of the inscription will be seen in Dr. Spiegelberg's chapter. The re-use of the stele by Merenptah is noticed in the next chapter.

In the brickwork of the long chambers north of Merenptah's temple, many of the bricks bear stamps of Amenhotep III., and not one was found of Merenptah. It appears, then, that the later king even obtained all his bricks by plundering the earlier temple.

The other works of Amenhotep III. have been described: the rearrangement of the temple of Amenhotep II., apparently to fit it for the worship of his daughter Sitamen, whose figure was found on one block; and the rebuilding of part of the chapel of Uazmes, as shown by the ring beneath the threshold.

CHAPTER V.

THE TEMPLE OF MERENPTAH.

25. As we have just noticed, in the previous chapter, the temple of Merenptah was constructed out of the materials of that of Amenhotep III. In this chapter, therefore, we shall ignore the details of the re-use of material and consider solely the work of Merenptah.

The plan of the temple is given in PL. XXV, which may be usefully compared with that of the Ramesseum. The great pylon in front has been entirely removed, and the only proof of it is the deep sand bed, bounded by brick walling above, and the sides of the pit cut in native marly Nile mud below. The levels from the water in February 1896 are:

Brick wall	.	.	.	.	.	174 inches
Native marl, or old Nile mud	.	.	105 ,,
Native sand	.	.	.	.	.	20 ,,
Water	.	.	.	.	.	0 ,,

This native mud is a thick bed of old Nile mud, deposited in prehistoric times when the Nile was subsiding from the far higher level which it had occupied. These high-level mud-beds are found in many parts of the country, such as on the plain by Kom Ombo, and on the plain of Tell el Amarna. Here, at Thebes, they are overlaid by very coarse gravels, as may be seen in the great scarp on the west of Tausert's temple. This shows that the Nile had subsided and run dry enough to deposit its mud, owing to lack of rainfall; and then had again risen with torrential rains which enabled it to carry down twenty feet thick of large gravels, many of the flints of which weigh several pounds. The section above exhibits this old Nile mud resting on native sand. The foundation pit is a great work, being 7 feet deep in native mud, with 6 feet more of walling above that, in all 13 feet deep, 208 feet long, and 37 feet wide; allowing about 15 or 20 inches of space around the stones, this would show a pylon base of 120 × 20 cubits. The Ramesseum pylon was 132 × 20 cubits. The sides were traced all along to the bottom, and the north quarter was completely turned over down to the native sand, in search of foundation deposits; but we found nothing. The passage-way leading to it at the north end between brick walls was evidently the entrance to the stairway of the pylon leading to the top; this stair is similarly at the north end of the Ramesseum pylon.

26. Passing the pylon we enter the front court, which had a colonnade of six pillars on either side; this was about two-thirds of the size of the Ramesseum court in each direction. It had an entrance in the south side, with two halls of four columns, and chambers at the side. The similar entrance in the Ramesseum had pillars of the same size, but twice as many in each direction. The perpendicular shading here on the east side of the wall of this entrance indicates a sloping foot to the wall at about 45°; the object of this was to prevent any use of the space between the wall and the pylon.

The second court appears to have had colonnades only on the front and back, and not at the sides. The bases for Osiride pillars remain along the west back, and a large square base on the north side appears as if it were for a statue.

From behind the row of Osiride pillars an exit in the south side led down steps to the great tank. This tank had probably been lined with stone, though now only the hole cut in the old Nile mud stratum remains. It was filled with washed-in earth, and, though we went down to water-level, we could not reach the bottom. The other tanks or sacred lakes are south of the temple at Karnak, and north of that at Koptos. None have been observed in connection with other funerary temples.

The third court was a hypostyle hall of twelve columns. Behind that was another hypostyle of eight columns, and chambers lay at the back of this and on either side.

27. The altar chamber was found at the N.W. corner. The base of the altar was not quite square, being in width 62·6N, 65·4E, 63·5S, 63·7W. The edge of the basement of it was 73·5, 76·6, 74·7, and 77·6 on corresponding sides. The sloping way up to it was 30·6 wide and 92·2 long, with a basement 39·4 wide. The angle of slope was indicated by the base line of a row of hieroglyphs remaining, with part of the signs *neheh*, showing that the inscription read down the slope; the angle was 1 on 4, giving a rise of 23 inches, which, with a step of about 10 inches at the lower end, would show a height of 33 inches for the altar. The slope was therefore merely formal, and was not actually used to ascend the altar.

This may be compared with the altar at Deir el Bahri, which is similarly in the N.W. corner of the site with a chamber behind it, a precisely analogous arrangement. The steps also slope up from the west. The steps at Deir el Bahri are 41 wide and 180 long, against 30·6 wide and 92 long here; they therefore served for actual ascent to the altar. The altar itself at Deir el Bahri was 193 × 153 inches, instead of only 63 inches square as here. Finding that in two temples, one of the earliest and one of the latest of this class, the altar is in the same position, we may look to the plans of other temples in search of the same feature. In the Ramesseum the large chamber Q of Lepsius, north of the hall E of Baedecker, might have been an altar court. In the temple of Sety at Qurneh a hall of columns on the north side has apparently in the middle of it two blocks of stone forming a square of 131 inches, which may well be the base of an altar (Denkmaler I, 86); and at Medinet Habu is a large hall in an analogous position, which might have contained an altar. It will be a point of investigation, in all future clearing of temples, to search for the altar chamber.

28. The mass of brick store-chambers on the north of the temple are preserved to a height of four or five feet in the middle, but are entirely denuded away at the N.W. corner. The long narrow space at the south side of this block was doubtless for a stairway, of which a few steps of brickwork yet remain. The columns in the hall which gives access to the western part of the block are 27·4 to 29·3 in diameter, some being slightly oval. A square abacus was found, 27·0 × 27·2 × 10 inches high. The distance between the abaci was 70 inches, according to the spacing on the architraves, which were 26·7 wide and 33·8 deep. This depth of the architrave was to allow of its appearing square beneath the arch of brickwork that rested on it. The spacing was thus:—

Top of architrave	33·8
Butment of brickwork	28·0
Inscription borders	{23·6 / to 3·9}
Lower edge	0

Thus, after 5·8 inches of the top were covered by the spring of the brick arch, the architrave appeared square in section, and with the inscription having an equal border above and below it. The roofing between the architraves was by brick arching, of which a fallen mass was found in the hall, three courses thick. From the measurements taken the inner diameter of this brick arch would have been 68 inches, and the thickness of the three courses is 28 inches. The breadth of the spaces between the architraves being 72, 56, and 68 inches, agrees to this width of arch.

Another piece of an architrave from this temple varies in size, being only 24·5 wide, but 39·0 deep. The spacing was thus:—

Top of architrave	39·0
(Brickwork	30·5)?
Inscription border	{27·3 / 3·2}
Lower edge	0

This was a wider band of inscription, and can hardly have belonged to this hall, but yet it is too narrow an architrave for any other columns that are known here. That it belonged to Merenptah appears from the hieroglyphs being exactly in the same style as his, and coloured dull blue in the same manner; but it was found in the Ramesseum as a re-used block in a restoration by Ramessu III. The line of brick butment is inserted on the supposition of leaving an equal border above and below the inscription, and that this architrave was designed to carry a brick arch appears from the extra height above the inscription. The bases of the columns are 49·7 across the top, 54·7 in the middle, and 15 high; they contract equally to the top and bottom. The inner lengths of these store galleries was evidently the designed part, as they are 610, 823, 418, 427 inches, or 30, 40, 20, 20 cubits of 20·3, 20·57, 20·9, 21·3 inches respectively. This gradual lengthening out of the cubit from west to east is curious. The widths of the galleries are 3 and 6 cubits of 20·6. The circle at the S.E. of the brick building is a granary. Nothing whatever was found in these galleries, not even any fallen roofing; hence it appears probable that they had wooden roofs, which were all removed for material in a short time.

At the southern entrance to the first court a capital still remains, of the bell or papyrus form. It is 27 inches wide at top, 18·7 at base, and the column 17·4 thick, while the height is 22 inches. This cannot have belonged to the columns remaining there, which are 33 thick on bases 77 wide in the inner vestibule, while the bases are 66 wide in the outer vestibule. There must therefore have been some smaller columns in this region.

Foundation deposits were searched for in the corners of the pylon site, under the corners of the foundations, and along most of the length of the foundations, and at the back corners of the temenos. Only a few blue beads, mostly wasters, from a factory, were found, and a few objects in coloured glaze, blue, red, and white (III, 28–34), with two small objects of sheet bronze (III, 35, 37). Most of these were in the trench west of the hall of eight columns, apparently at the entrance to the cella.

29. The greatest discovery in the temple was that of the black granite stele of Merenptah, engraved on the back of the stele of Amenhotep III, which lay in the S.W. corner of the first court. It had evidently stood against the south wall in the corner, and been overthrown forwards. It rested on the base of the column at its east side. This stele has been described among the works of Amenhotep III, and its inscription, which is of the greatest value, not only for the Israel campaign, but also for the other places named in Syria and for the Libyan war, is fully treated by Dr. Spiegelberg in this volume. The photograph of the inscription is given on PL. XIII, and the facsimile copy of the inscription on PL. XIV.

Portions of two colossal seated statues of Merenptah in black granite were found at the back of the second court. They had probably stood on pedestals, one on each side of the axis. The lower part of one was found, and this was left in place; but the upper part of the other statue was brought away to the Cairo Museum. It gives the best portrait known of Merenptah (PL. VI, 10, 11). The colour is still fresh upon it, yellow on the head-dress, red on the lips, white and black in the eyes. This was, next to the Israel inscription, the greatest prize of the year.

In the ruins of the first court was also found a small tablet of limestone with fresh colouring on it, representing Pen-rannut adoring an official named Ptah-hes. A few ostraka with inscriptions were found, mainly at the south entrance to the first court (XX, 8–13); and some hieratic quarry marks are found upon the blocks of stone in the foundations (IX, 14–23). Both of these classes are discussed by Dr. Spiegelberg.

CHAPTER VI.

THE TEMPLE OF TAUSERT.

30. The site of this temple is in a levelled area, which has been cut into the sloping mass of Nile gravels, leaving a steep scarp along the north and west sides of the area. This area was levelled for some other purpose earlier than this temple, as the temple is not square with it, and a part of the west scarp has been cut away to admit of the N.W. corner of the temple. See General Plan, PL. XXII, and Wall Plan, PL. XXVI.

Of the building of the temple only a few stones of the foundation remained, between the deposits marked II and VIII on the Plan, PL. XXVI; otherwise the only evidences of it were the foundation trenches cut in the gravel and marl ground, to a depth of about five feet, and filled with clean sand. These trenches were all cleared in search of foundation deposits, except a part at the back of the cella, which was deep in accumulated dust and chips from tombs cut in the scarp above it.

The general plan of the temple is much like Merenptah's. There is the thick pylon, which here seems to have been hollow, so that no foundation was cut in the middle of it. This pylon would have been 110 × 20 or 24 cubits, against 120 × 20 in Merenptah's, or 132 × 20 in the Ramesseum. Next is the first court, which was here 75 × 50 cubits, just the same size as that of Merenptah. In place, however, of a second large court and two hypostyle halls, there are here only three small halls, not as large as the smallest of those of Merenptah. Behind these is the cella and chambers on either side of it. Owing to the greater number of small chambers (in lieu of the brick storerooms of Merenptah), the actual area of stone building of Tausert is, however, equal to that of Merenptah.

31. The foundation deposits were the most valuable result attained here. They were placed at the two back corners (V and VI, PL. XXVI), along the side walls (III and IV), and at the main cross wall (I and II), and under the doorways (VII and VIII). No system or order was traceable in the positions of the objects. In general it seems that the large block of stone with cartouches was laid down in the trench upon a wide mat, sometimes with the copper models of tools beneath it, and a heap of small glazed objects were poured out over it. The region of each deposit was indicated by blue glazed beads scattered in the sand around.

The numbers of each object found in the deposits, with references to the Plates, are as follow:—

	Deposit I	Deposit II	Deposit III	Deposit IV	Deposit V	Deposit VI	Deposit VII	Deposit VIII	Total
Pl. XVI:—									
1	3	2	6	30	1	19	13	7	81
2	2	..	2	16	3	14	7	9	53
3	9	6	2	8	0	5	21	2	59
4	oval	..	4	oval	..	..	..	..	
5	13	8	2	9	4	10	16	6	68
6	1	..	2	16	..	15	7	10	55
7	9	4	16	42	..	49	34	10	165
8	32	20	27	52	38	24	31	23	247
9	2	..	1	1	3	3	7	2	29
10	15	16	15	42	17	29	14	15	163
11	22	14	7	12	23	7	52	9	146
12	33	22	16	53	30	27	7	48	236
13	..	8	..	..	..	..	..	..	8
14	5	7	3	1	7	..	6	..	23
15	2	1	..	1	1	1	1	..	16
" plain	4	2	..	4	..	1	1	..	12
16	17	7	7	4	14	4	21	1	75
17	9	5	1	..	..	2	6	..	33
18	7	15	4	8	..	6	11	5	67
19	16	25	11	37	21	13	7	29	159
20, 21	4	4	..	..	3	16	7	9	43
22	13	..	..	26	16	..	14	37	106
23	1	..	..	1	..	..	..	..	2
24	..	..	1	..	..	1	..	..	1
25	..	1	..	..	..	..	..	..	4
26	..	..	..	..	..	6	..	..	6
27	..	..	..	..	..	7	..	..	7
28-30	..	..	..	..	..	3	1	2	6
31	1	1	..	1	..	6	1	..	9
32	1	..	..	..	..	5	1	..	7
33	..	1	..	1	..	1	1	..	1
34	..	..	..	..	..	6	..	1	8
35	1	..	..	3	..	10	4	..	19
36	..	1	..	..	..	..	..	..	1
37	..	..	..	..	..	1	..	..	1
38	..	..	..	..	1	1	..	1	3
39	..	..	..	..	..	1	..	..	1
40	..	..	..	..	..	..	..	..	
Pl. XVII:—									
1	..	..	..	..	1	..	..	..	1
2	..	..	..	1	..	1	..	..	5

Incomplete.

Of these deposits the first three are incompletely recorded, owing to the thefts by the local workmen. After I had discharged them, and used men and boys from a distance, I believe nothing whatever was abstracted. Unfortunately these thefts vitiate any conclusions about the total quantities of each type. From what I saw afterwards I suppose that the first three deposits were about of the same average richness as the others. One point is pretty clear, that there were an equal number of the bulls' heads and haunches of the full type (8, 12), and probably equal numbers of the full type of sacrificed ox (10), the flat type of bull's head (11), and the flower (19). But it is obvious in the complete deposits that no precise numbers were set aside for each, though in some cases there is roughly the same proportion of different objects. This looks as if all the glazed objects had been put in a basket, mixed together, and then turned out by the handful at the ceremony of the foundation. Many of the objects having been broken anciently when buried shows that they had been roughly treated.

32. Some notes may be made upon the objects drawn here. In Pl. XVI the scarabs Nos. 1 and 7 are all moulded and not worked by hand; they are made in two pieces, a thick back in which a groove is made for a hole from end to end, and a thin face which in several cases has split off the back. The colour has in all cases been blue; but those in damper parts of the site at the west end, where the ground was deeper, are more or less whitened and decomposed. The square plaques, Nos. 2, 4, 6, are also moulded in two pieces stamped on both sides, with a groove in one piece to provide a hole from end to end. The colour of all of these, and of the scarabs, is a very brilliant indigo blue, when in good preservation. The long plaques, 3 and 5, are plain on the back, being simply pressed in a mould; they are white, blue, and dark violet. The cartouches are also found on some figures of fish, 15, of ox haunches, 14, and on rings, 21. The models of ox heads (11, 12), haunches (8, 13, 14), and bound oxen (9, 10) are of two kinds: some in high relief, well rounded (8, 10, 12), others flat in form and marked out with mere lines (9, 11, 13, 14). The tied-up birds (18) are like those at Tell el Amarna: some examples are of blue glaze, others white, and some violet. The same variety of colour is found in the examples of the lotus flower, 16. The flower 19 has been supposed to be a hand, but the earlier type in the Ramesseum and Merenptah's deposits shows it to be a flower.

THE TEMPLE OF TAUSERT.

Turning to the metal objects, they are all made in thin sheet copper, to judge by their softness and absence of corrosion. The piece 23 looks as if it were a model ingot, cast in that form for convenience of lifting it and of securing it on animals in travelling; the four lugs serve as handles by which two or four men could lift it, and also for securing it by rope lashing. The same form is known in the ingot of tin found at Falmouth, weighing 158 lbs. and therefore needing four men to lift it about readily (*Evans, Ancient Bronze*, fig. 514). No actual ingots have been yet found in Egypt, so far as I remember. The two handled dishes 24, 25, probably represent mortar trays. The long slips, 26, 27, seem to be crowbars, as several were uniformly bent up at one end; these show then the only crowbars yet known from Egypt. The hoes, 28, 29, 30, are of the type well known in later Egyptian bronze, where the flat sheet of metal is wrapped round the handle. The axe, 31, is of the usual type; as are also the adze, 32, and knife, 33. The knife with a spur on it, 34, is a new form, the meaning of which is obscure. The mortise chisel, 35, and flat chisel, 36, are of the usual forms. The ebony cramp, 37, is a model of the wooden cramps used for linking together the stones of a building, and bears the cartouche with the title *Neb taui*. The two model corn grinders of yellow quartzite have the *nefer* signs and a border line painted on in black. A piece of red glass, 39, is partly decomposed to yellow; what it represents is unknown.

Besides these small objects there were also in five of the deposits a block of sandstone (XVII, 2) bearing the two cartouches of Tausert carefully engraved. And in one deposit a brick of coarse mortar (XVII, 1) which has been stamped with the cartouche; it has been laid in the hole while soft, and pressed out of shape, and further trodden upon. Many jars were found, as fig. 5, and some bowls and pans, figs. 8, 9, 10; a large number of little cups, figs. 4, 6, were in most of the deposits; and a few handles of jars are also drawn here, for the sake of dated types. Some of the potsherds bear inscriptions, which were written on them as datings of wine, when the jars were in use (XIX, 1–4). Of animal offerings there was a calf's haunch in deposits 1, 4, and 6; and a calf's head in deposits 4 and 6; a pigeon's head in deposit 6, and a pigeon in deposit 1. In deposit 7 was a thick bed of leaves of a tree mixed with beads above the glazed objects, and the copper models of tools lay on the top of the leaves.

We now turn to consider the name and position of the builder of this temple. At first the resemblance of the cartouches to those of Ramessu II led us to think that they were variants of that king; but it seemed plain when examined that these names belong to a queen, for on XVI, 1, 2, 5, and XVII, 2, we have clearly *sit*, not *si ra*. And on the cartouche in XVI, 3, 6, 7 and XVII, 2 there is clearly *t* and not *ra* at the top, and over the *sotep;* and the seated figure has not the feather of Maat but the double crown of Mut; hence it cannot be attributed to Ramessu II. The date of this deposit is nearly fixed by the wine jar inscriptions found in it being of Sety II; and hence it is almost certainly a very short time after that reign. Now the important queen Tausert comes next after Sety II, as queen of Siptah; and we can hardly refuse to read here therefore in the cartouches, *Ta-user-t : sotep-n-Mut : sit-ra : mery-amen*. The form of the cartouches is manifestly copied from those of Ramessu II, and ingeniously adapted as a parody or imitation of what was already so utterly familiar to the eyes of every Egyptian in those times. Now that this new cartouche is definitely established by all these instances, we can see that a few other examples of it may have been previously misplaced as being of Ramessu II, one for certain from Gurob ("Kahun" XXIII, 50).

33. Here we may well observe the question of the relation of the reign of this queen to that of Siptah her husband. Here in this temple there is no evidence of Siptah; nor can the objects have been made at the same time as the foundation deposits of Siptah, as there are differences throughout in the colour and form of every class of object. Was then her independent reign, and this temple, before or after that of Siptah? There is most conclusive evidence in the 4th deposit of Siptah, as there was found a scarab of Tausert, like XVI, 7, different in fabric and colour from those scarabs of Siptah, but like those of Tausert. It is evident that this is a stray scarab of the large batch made for the Tausert temple. Unless then we imagine that Siptah's deposit was opened beneath his walls to insert a later scarab, or that Tausert's scarabs were made in a different style by anticipation and kept for subsequent use in her temple—either of which suppositions would be very wild and forced—we must grant that a stray scarab of the earlier batch made for Tausert had been left over at the factory or office of works and was put in with the later batch made for Siptah. The style of the Tausert deposits is moreover certainly intermediate between those of Ramessu II,

and those of Siptah, and therefore probably before the latter.

We are led therefore to see that Tausert reigned alone as an independent queen, and that later on the chief seal-bearer Bay elevated Siptah, who married Tausert to legitimate his position. There are three scarabs known of Tausert as queen, one in Turin (mis-read as Ta isit, owing to being broken, Hist. Scarabs, 1998), one in Mr. MacGregor's collection, and one which I exchanged thence to my own series.

The whole question of the history of the changes shown in the successive usurpations of tomb XIV in the Tombs of the Kings will have to be re-studied with this new evidence in hand. If, as is stated, it is there shown that Tausert alone (in the form there shown) succeeded Siptah we should have to arrange the history thus. 1st Tausert alone, copying Ramessu II. 2nd Tausert, wife of Siptah. 3rd Tausert alone, as royal wife. The strange cartouche given in Lepsius' Denkmaler iii 206 b should also be re-examined. If it is not restored by Lepsius it is possible that it reads, *Sit-ra; Amen mery sit* (i.e. *Mery-amen, sit-amen*); the latter part being like the second cartouche on the block here (XVII, 2). Or possibly it might be copied from Siptah and read, *Akhet-ra; Amen-mery (Ra) sit*.

CHAPTER VII.

THE TEMPLE OF SIPTAH.

34. To the north of the temple of Amenhotep II, between that and the temple of Tahutmes III, is a small temple site of closely the same character as that of Tausert. As I walked over the ground I eyed the long foundation trenches cut in the gravel, and filled with sand; and so soon as we had finished the site of Amenhotep II, we attacked this. It proved to be a little temple of just the same work as that of Tausert, but much smaller. The foundation deposits proved it to be of Siptah, her husband.

In plan, Pl. XXVI, the temple appears not to have had any thick pylon, only a front wall. Inside there were apparently two hypostyle halls. The first 40 × 25 cubits, had four rows of three columns each; the second two ranks of four columns. A few store chambers stood at the sides. Behind this was the cella, and some small chambers round it. The whole was on a very modest scale, as compared with the earlier temples; and it can hardly have been more imposing than the chapels of Uazmes or the white queen.

35. The foundation deposits were found at eight places, analogous to those of Tausert; and, like those, there were none found to the east of the main cross wall, across the middle of the temple. The objects, shown in Pls. XVII, 13–23, and XVIII, were not so irregularly placed as those of Tausert. Some definite rules could be fixed as to the positions of the blocks of stone with cartouches of the king and those with the name of the Chancellor Bay. These blocks were always face up, side by side, with bases to the east and tops west; and Siptah's was nearest to the corner, with Bay next to it away from the corner. The calf's head was placed on or off the stones, any way; the haunch was on or off the stones, any way; the mortars were always upright, and close around the stones. The large pans of pottery were at a higher level and put on the inner side of the stones, The small glazed objects were poured out upon the stones and had run down at the side.

The glazing is much poorer than that of Tausert, and is of a dull pea-green, instead of the brilliant indigo blue. The workmanship is also rougher and more careless. The plaques (XVIII, 1, 2) are made in two pieces like those of Tausert; the scarab, 3, and the square-ended scarab, 4, are also made with the back and face separately. Thin gold-foil plaques also bear the cartouches of the king (8, 9). Rings are far commoner here than they are with Tausert; they bear the cartouches of Siptah (5, 6), the motto "established for all years" (7), the wish "Amen open a good new year" (14), and a multitude of figures of gods and emblems 15·35). Besides Siptah, the great Chancellor Bay also appears in these deposits; thin gold foil plaques impressed with his name are found (10), also rings of his (11, 12) and square-ended scarabs of his (13). The ox haunch and head (36, 38) and the bound ox for sacrifice (37) appear here, as with Tausert; but there are none of the fishes, ducks, and flowers which were made before. The models of tools are much the same as those of Tausert (42–57); pieces of a blue glazed vase (39) bear the name of Siptah, like the larger blue vases with the Ramesside names in the Louvre. The hemidisc of alabaster (41) is of a form known in other deposits. A similar but larger piece was produced by the diggers as having been found between deposits III and VI in the foundations of Tausert: as it bore the cartouche of Ramessu II in black ink I felt some doubt as to their good faith, and have not included it among Tausert's deposits.

In the corners of Siptah's foundations were placed

pairs of blocks of sandstone (XVII, 11, 12) bearing the cartouches of Siptah, and the titles and name of the Chancellor Bay, whose importance at this period is already well known from other monuments. Here we find him acting as coequal with the king in the founding of the royal temple. The deposit VIII, which had been exposed by denudation and scattered, is doubtless the source of the block of Siptah which is in the Marseille museum, described by Maspero in his catalogue (1889) as No. 36 ; in size, material, and workmanship it is identical with the blocks from the temple. In the deposits were many rough mortars and pestles of sandstone (15), pairs of corn grinders (13, 14), rough red-brown pottery jars (18), dishes (19, 20), and little cups (16, 17). Tall stands for supporting trays (21, 22) were in some deposits, and most of the deposits had one large wine jar (23) with inscription.

The actual numbers of objects found are as follows :—

	Deposit I.	Deposit II.	Deposit III.	Deposit IV.	Deposit V.	Deposit VI.	Deposit VII.	Total.
PL. XVIII. :—								
1	3, 27	2	..	3	3	} 7	6	92
2	6, 25	3	1	3	3			
3	1	1	5	4	10	..	..	23
4	..	7	4	6	12	3?	8?	40
5	11	11	11	19	37	} ..	40?	206
6	4	11	19	15	28			
7	2	2	..	..	..	..	..	4
8	11	10	..	4	7			
Silver	3	..	..	..	..	18?	18	126
9	11	6	1	7	5			
10	16	3	..	2	4			
11, 12	3	5	7	6	16	..	4?	41
13	1	1	2	..	5	1?	2?	12
14	..	..	..	..	..	..	..	1
15, 16	..	1	3	1	5	{rings 95	rings 37	rings 262
17–20	2	9	10	7	14			
21	..	3	2	2	1			
22	..	4	..	..	..			
23	4	2	1	3	7			
24, 25	..	1	..	..	..			
26	1	3	..	..	..			
27	..	..	..	..	1			
28	1	..	..	1	1			
29	..	..	1	1	1			
30, 31, 32	1	4	6	4	10			
33	..	..	1	..	1			
34	..	..	..	3	4			
35	..	..	2	1	1			
36	92	45	28	31	68	26	47	337
37	84	31	31	21	52	26	40	283
38	93	36	23	24	71	31	36	314
39	..	..	..	1?	..	..	..	1
40	..	..	..	..	{agate limestone}	agate	quartz	4
41	..	..	1	..	..	..	..	1
42, 43	..	..	..	..	..	2	..	2
44	10	1	..	..	..	..	..	11
45	3	..	..	..	..	..	..	3
46, 47, 48	4	..	..	..	..	..	..	4
49	14	..	..	..	..	..	..	14
PL. XVIII.—continued :—								
50	2	1	..	4	..	..	1	8
51	5	2	..	..	..	..	..	7
52	9	..	..	18	7	14	10	58
53	8	3	3	3	..	..	4	21
54, 55	2	2	..	..	2	..	1	7
56	..	..	..	..	1	..	..	1
57	1	..	..	1	..	..	..	2
PL. XVII. :—								
11	..	1	1	1	1	1	1	6
12	..	1	1	1	1	1	1	6
13, 14	..	8	12	10	n.	4	n.	50?
15	..	8	10	10	n.	4	n.	50?
18	5	3	2	..	..	..	3	
20	4	1	..	2	..	..	..	
23	..	..	1	1	1	1	1	5
PL. XVI :—								
23	..	..	..	..	..	1	1	2

There were also many silver foil plaques, as 8 to 10, indistinct (11 in I, 1 in II, 8 in IV, and 4 in V) ; 4 indistinct gold foils, and a copper foil in I. A few types of rings are not drawn, as the scorpion, frog, crocodile, and uaz sceptre; in IV there was a scarab of Tausert, and some hundreds of rough chipped beads of carnelian. The deposit VIII was all broken up and scattered many years ago, and the block of Siptah from that is now at Marseille. There does not appear to be any regularity in the numbers of various objects in each deposit, and it is probable therefore that the glazed things were all put in a basket, and some handfuls of the mixed varieties were poured out on the cartouche stones.

CHAPTER VIII.

LATER OBJECTS AND GENERAL PLAN.

36. As all the temples which have been here described were destroyed soon after they were built, very few objects of later date were found in them. This history was different from that of the Ramesseum, which for stores and for funeral chapels continued in use for many centuries. A small altar of offerings came from the Ramesseum (VIII, 2) dedicated to Osiris for Du-se-nub. The lower square of inscription is on the edge of the slab.

Some excellent drawings on pottery were left behind by a school of artists in the Ramesseum brick galleries. A girl's head has been very carefully drawn (VI, 14) and finished off with red cheeks ; but a rival student took it up and added, with a different brush, the dog scratching her nose. A good head of a king below appears to be that of Ramessu IV; and the head of a royal sphinx is probably of the same

D

king. Another admirable piece of rough drawing was found in the brick chambers north of the pylon of Tahutmes IV (VI, 17); it shows a young peasant going out on his way in the world, with his swag on his back, the delightful *gauche* rusticity of his upturned face and lank hair is one of the best sketches of character that has been found.

37. One of the most prominent landmarks of the western side of Thebes is a piece of brick wall that stands on the hill between the temple of Tahutmes IV and the great scarp around the temple of Tausert. This wall is part of the back of the forecourt of a large private tomb, the plan of which is shewn on PL. XXVI as the tomb of Khonsuardus. The three tomb wells shown in the three back chambers were cleared out. In them were some pieces of painted coffins. The better and earlier was finely written, and covered with clear dark-brown varnish; from the fragments I could recover the name of Khonsuardus, goldsmith of the temple of Amen. The other coffin was coarsely painted without any varnish, in the cold, hard style of the early XXVIth dynasty, and bore the name of Psamtek. It seems, then, that Khonsuardus was the temple jeweller at the close of the XXVth or beginning of the XXVIth dynasty, and a son of his was buried here also in the XXVIth dynasty. Probably the wells were for separate graves; but the chambers have been all broken through below, and the contents broken up and mixed together.

38. The scarp behind the temple of Tausert is cut through the thick bed of coarse Nile gravels, down to the level of a bed of ancient Nile mud below them. While that mud was still soft, the gravel bed has slid down several feet toward the Nile, making a great slickenside beneath the gravels, and leaving large gaps between them and the mud below. This place offered a most tempting position to excavate tombs, and most of the mud bed has been removed, so that the upper gravel bed has very little support left. These tombs vary from single small chambers, to three or four chambers with an outer court wall. The most important of them had a long flight of steps, going 171 inches horizontally, and steeply inclined, a doorway at the bottom opened into a chamber 114 × 86 inches, from which opened out another chamber 104 × 92 inches. We cleared out nearly all of these tombs, but only found a few amulets and a poor set of canopic jars of about the XXIIIrd dynasty. One tomb was filled with bones of oxen.

39. Just below the scarp north of Tausert's temple, not far from the corner, were remains of a brick chamber built against the face of the cutting. In this were found many iron tools and some bronze objects. Beside those shewn in the photograph, PL. XXI, an important piece was stolen by the finder, which I can only describe from the sight of it which a friend of mine had at Thebes. I had hoped that perhaps the inspector of the Department of Antiquities, whom we had to pay, might have been of some use to preserve things; but, on the contrary, he was on the most cordial terms with the dealers, and never prevented anything being stolen. The trumpet which was taken had an inscription on it, "Asar-hapi gives life to Pekh-ar-Khonsu, son of Du-amen-neb-nest-taui, son of Hor." This inscription gives the best indication that we have as to the date of these things. Hor and Du-amen-neb-nest-taui are both pretty common names during two or three centuries before the XXVIth dynasty. The other name gives a still closer indication, as it is not so common; it occurs in this form (excepting the duck *p* for the mat *p*) in a husband of a woman Shep mut (stele Turin, Lieblein, Dict. Nom., 1294); and it occurs with the mat *p*, as here, on a bronze vase in the Louvre, where the man is son of a Psemthek (Pierret, Inscr. Louvre, II, 121); but in no case has the name the seated lioness determinative to *pekh*, as here. These instances point to the end of the XXVth dynasty (Shep-mut), or the close of the reign of Psemthek I. As the name Du-amenneb-nest-taui seems hardly so late as the XXVIth dynasty, we might put this trumpet to somewhere between 680 and 630 B.C., or possibly anywhere within the VIIth century.

Turning now to the photograph PL. XXI, it will be seen that the largest object is a bronze helmet, the form of which is wholly un-Egyptian. But such a helmet is constantly found on the Assyrian sculptures of the VIIIth century B.C. And we are led therefore to look to the Assyrian occupation of Thebes by Esarhaddon between 672 and 670 B.C.; the later invasion by Nebuchadnezzar a century afterwards in 572 B.C. is too late for the style of names which here occur. The bronze bowl below the helmet is of a usual form, and shows nothing further.

40. This foreign origin for these things is confirmed when we look at the iron tools and see that they are mostly of forms which were unknown to the Egyptians. Large quantities of iron tools were found at Khorsabad, and were therefore probably of about 700 B.C., or the first half of the VIIth century, which would agree to the common use of iron tools,

LATER OBJECTS AND GENERAL PLAN.

as here indicated about 670 B.C., by the Assyrian army. When we remember that the Chalybes in the highlands of Armenia lived by iron-working in the time of Xenophon, and continue still to make iron to the present day, it seems that we there see the most likely direction for the supply of the iron so abundantly used in Assyria, when as yet it seems to have been unknown to the Egyptians. We will now notice the forms of these tools in detail.

The sickle, at the top left hand, has two rivet-holes for a handle.

The mortise chisel, below that, has a slope on either face, the edge view being shown here; it was evidently for use with a mallet, as there is a wide stop or flange on both faces to prevent it being driven too deep into the handle; and one of the ferrules seems by the size to belong to this.

The file, between the chisel and sickle, is shaped like a very thick-backed knife, hatched all over both sides by cuts from a chisel. It must evidently have been used as a file, as there is no edge for it to cut with as a knife; but it is the earliest stage of the triangular saw-file, when only two faces were hatched across, and the third had not widened out equal to the others.

The rasp at the bottom left hand is made precisely like a modern rasp except in the irregularity of the punching; the flat form, thinning out to the end, with a good tang, but no flange, and squared-up sides and end, shows that the best type was already fixed on in this earliest example.

The crank pieces next to that are both made with the long ends squared to fit into wood, and the short ends finished to a conical point. As there are several brace-bits here, it is evident that some kind of a brace was probably in use; and these crank pieces seem certainly to have been fittings for a brace of some kind. How it was arranged we cannot yet see, in the absence of any of the woodwork.

The centre-bits next to these are not far from the types of modern times, and are almost exactly what are now used by the Algerians. The two edges are alike in form, both being scrapers, and are not differenced as a cutter on one side and a scraper on the other, as they are in modern tools. The square shank is evidently for fitting them interchangeably into a handle, or more probably a brace.

The scoop cutter between them and the bowl is an admirable tool for drilling hard wood; the twisted S-shaped section of it turns the edge on each side forward in the direction of cutting. This shows that a negative rotation was used in work; the same is shown by the smaller centre-bit, while the larger centre-bit was for positive rotation, as modern tools.

On the right-hand side of the plate are two chisels. The wide one has an equal slope on each side; the large oblong ferrule placed with it, clearly can only belong to it, and proves that it had a wooden handle, and was not a hard edge for an anvil, which it resembles. The smaller chisel has the slope all on one side, like a modern chisel; and it is narrow in proportion to its depth, like a mortising chisel. The ferrule, placed above, does not clearly fit any of the tools here; it might have gone on either the rasp or the sickle handle. At the top right hand is a small punch.

The saws are of the Eastern type, to cut when pulling and not when pushing. There is no appreciable set in the teeth to alternate sides in order to clear the way in cutting; but the rake of the teeth toward the handle is obvious in the longest saw, implying the pulling cut.

As an approximate test of the softness of the iron, the question of magnetisation was tried, using a powerful electro-magnet, and giving a blow to the tool when on it, and again when off it, before testing by a compass needle. The result was that the two crank pieces were quite soft iron. The very wide chisel was soft at the tang and the greater part of the length, but magnetised at the edge. The rasp and sickle were slightly magnetised, and moderately hard. The three saws, the two mortise chisels, the file, the two centre-bits, the scoop drill, and the little punch, proved to be all of them permanently magnetised, even after repeated blows in different directions.

41. The general plan, PL. XXII, shows the relative positions of all of the temples described here. As the exact details are given in the larger plans of each site separately, the small plans in this plate have been freely restored, where the symmetry of parts showed what must have existed. These are therefore the best plans for comparison together to observe questions of arrangements and size. The exact bearing of each temple was a special point of observation. To ascertain this, a long line was adopted running N. and S., defined by marks on a brick vault of the Ramesseum, the E. face of the high wall of Khonsuardus, and a wall face standing up against the sky line at Medinet Habu. Then a theodolite was set up at each temple site exactly in this sight line, and the angle between the sight line and the best defined line

of the temple ruin was observed. In the evening of the same day, Polaris and Canopus were observed, to ascertain the true bearing of the sight line. First taking Polaris twice, and Canopus as a time star between the two; and then reversing every part of the theodolite (which was not a transit), and repeating these three observations. This gave a result safe within 2′, and much more exact than the fixing of the temple axes. The magnetic variation thus observed was 4° 55′ W. of N. on 16 Feb., 1897.

The observed axes of the temples have all had corrections applied to them to reduce from the observed line to the best mean axis in each case, as measured from the plans. The results are as follows, arranging them in the order of the azimuths: 123° here means, 123° from true N. round by E., or 33° S. of E.

Merenptah				about 1200 B.C.	123° 24′ ± 15′
Tausert				,, 1180 ,,	124° 7′ ± 20′
Tahutmes IV.				,, 1420 ,,	129° 55′ ± 15′
Siptah				,, 1180 ,,	130° 57′ ± 30′
Scarp of rock				?	131° 8′ ± 30′
Khuenaten				,, 680 ,,	131° 15′ ± 30′
Uasmes				,, 1550 ,,	131° 32′ ± 10′
Rameses II.				,, 1280 ,,	132° 27′ ± 5′
White queen				?	133° 0′ ± 1°
Rameses III.				,, 1180 ,,	137° 25′ ± 15′
Amenhotep II.				,, 1440 ,,	139° 19′ ± 20′

These have a very great value for the question of any astronomical reference in the axes of temples. Here is a group of ten temples and chapels, all for one purpose, and therefore to be expected to point to one star; all with the same distant horizon, so that uncertainties cannot come in from that cause, and all built by one school of architects. If ever we could expect to find the astronomical reference in any case, it should be in such a series of connected buildings. Yet there seems no trace of a sequence of change in direction along with the time. The dates here given go to and fro in the most indifferent fashion, and show no connection whatever with the changes of direction.

CHAPTER IX.

THE INSCRIPTIONS.

By Dr. WILHELM SPIEGELBERG.

42. PLATE I, XVIIIth DYNASTY. Fig. 1. The signs above the front figure probably give his name, *Aa . kheper . ka . ra . teku*, and the title *hen . ka* "the *ka* priest"; but this is not quite certain in the present broken state. Perhaps *teku* may be separate from the king's name, and on comparison with Fig. 2, where the compounded royal name has no cartouche, this is the more likely. It might be asked if *teku* is not a mistake for *tekenu*, the human sacrifice discussed with much insight by M. Maspero in the tomb of Mentuhikhopeshef (Mem. Miss. Arch. Fr. V 438 f.f.). Unfortunately there is not enough of the scene to show if it was one of human sacrifice. Fig. 2 shows a priest of Amen, and a man named *Aa . kheper . ka . ra . senb*. Both pieces are evidently from one tomb of the time of Tahutmes I, which had been broken up for building material under Tahutmes IV.

Fig. 3. A tablet showing a woman, *Baket*, sacrificing to "Hathor lady of heaven, mistress of the two lands." Below is the dedication, with some orthographic blunders, to "Hathor, lady of heaven, mistress of the gods, that she may give milk, oxen, geese, and all good and pure things to the *ka* of the engraver of Amen, *Amen . em . het*. His beloved wife, the mistress of the house, *Baket*."

Fig. 4. Part of an altar inscribed "The first prophet of Tahutmes III, *Ra* says, 'Hail to thee *Ra* in thy rising, hidden in thy setting. Beautiful in thy shining . . . on the back of thy mother. Thou shinest as king of the cycle of nine gods. Thou makest (*dry* [*k?*]) [life?] to every one (*her neb?*). The goddess of truth embraces thee always. Thou coursest through (*nemtak*) the heaven, thy heart being glad. The sea of the two swords has become . . . . . his arms . . . . . !'" The prophet named here is known also by another inscription (L.D. iii, 62b), where he has the titles "high priest of Amen in the tomb-temple of Tahutmes III, *Ra*" (see Spiegelberg in Rec. Trav. xix, 87).

Fig. 5. A fragment of the splendid hard limestone colossus of Amenhotep III, reading "lord of the lands in . . . ."

Fig. 6. Part of a limestone tablet with figures of "The lady of the house, *Nefret . ári*," "His daughter . . . ," "The son *Pendua*," "His son *Nen*," "His son *Pendeh*[*u*]*et*." The latter name means "the man of the goddess *Dehnet*," who is a form of the goddess of the Theban necropolis, *Meritsegret*.

Fig. 7. A sandstone tablet with Tahutmes IV before a god, probably Amen. The end of inscription remaining is *redát mu* "giving water," showing that the king was offering water. Below is, "For I have settled (*gerget na*) the fortress of Tahutmes IV among the tribes of Palestine [with everything] his majesty took in the town of Qaza . . . . ." Perhaps "Tahutmes IV among the tribes of Palestine" is the

THE INSCRIPTIONS.

proper name of the fortress, like one names "Tahutmes III the encloser of the Sati" (Annals, L.D. iii, 32, line 21). The name Qaza ... might be conjecturally restored, Qa-za-ua-da-na (Müller, *Asien und Europa*, 335), a vassal land of the king of the Khita; here it might be a town of the land of Qa-za-uada-na, the well-known "town of the Kanaan" is a parallel to this.

Fig. 8. Sandstone tablet of "The good god Tahutmes IV endowed with life" before "Amen-Ra lord of heaven" offering bread. Amen says, "I have settled the vile Kush, I have guided his majesty in his victories." If the construction of these parallel inscriptions is treated aright here, these tablets were dedicated in the temple of Tahutmes IV in honour of his victories in Syria and Ethiopia.

43. PLATE II, Fig. 1. Wooden ushabti of Nehi, the well-known viceroy of Ethiopia, under Tahutmes III, with the usual text, "O, thou figure, if the viceroy of Ethiopia Nehi is ordered to do works that are done there in the nether world as it is his duty (?), to cultivate the fields, to irrigate the banks, to carry the sand of the east to the west, [say] I am here!"

Fig. 2. Part of an ushabti figure (?) inscribed, "[Lord] of the two lands, Tahutmes I, beloved of Amen of Karnak."

Fig. 3 is an alabaster figure of Amenhotep II from his temple.

Plate III, Figs. 1, 2, 3, 5. "The good god Amenhotep II, beloved of Amen."

Fig. 4. "The good god Amenhotep II, endowed with life."

Fig. 19. Part of a glazed tube gives to Amenhotep III the title, "beloved of the cycle of nine gods of the royal jubilees." This jubilee is named also on Figs. 14 ("great in jubilees"), 15 ("rich in jubilees"), and 16, 18.

Fig. 23. Wine stamp of limestone, reading, "Wine of the west river," that is, the Canopic branch of the Nile. (Brugsch. Geog. 88).

Fig. 24. A stamp cut in pottery reading, "House of Aten."

Fig. 25. "Aa . kheperu . ra shining upon the throne of Ra." This scarab was probably made in honour of the coronation day of Amenhotep II, for *kha* seems —amongst other meanings—to be used for the enthronement of a king.

Fig. 26. Prenomen of Amenhotep III.

Fig. 27. "The divine wife of Amon ..."

44. PLATE V. Fig. 5. "Amenhotep II." Fig. 6. "Year 26, Vine dresser Pinchas."

PLATE VIII. Fig. 1. Piece of a rude stele, with "the good god Tahutmes IV" adoring a Syrian war goddess on horseback. I should be inclined to think, from existing indications, that this is the goddess Asit (Müller, *Asien und Europa*, 316).

Fig. 2. Table of offerings. Left hand, "Offering which the king gives to Osiris Khentamenti, the Great God, Lord of Abydos, that he may give all offerings, all provisions, all good and pure things to the Osiris Tås-nub, the deceased." Right hand, "Offering which the king gives to Osiris Un-nefer the Great God, the Prince of Eternity, that he may give all offerings, all provisions, and all good and pure things to the *ka* of the Osiris Tås-nub the deceased." Below is the full title, "The Osiris, singer of the harim (*hes khenu*) Tås-nub." Usually the title is singer of the harim of Amen, and that might be lost in the erasure, if written with *n* in an oval. As this title only occurs in this orthography between the XXIInd and XXVIth dynasty, so far as I know, it would give an approximate age for the tablet.

Fig. 3. A tablet, found in the temple of Merenptah, "made by the watchman of the temple of millions of years (the Ramesseum) Pen-rannut, the deceased, of Thebes," who adores "the able spirit of *Ptah-hes*," who is seated before him.

Fig. 4. Tablet held by a kneeling figure, in grey granite, "Praise to Ra in [his] rising ... till his setting in the west, [by] the royal scribe Sesh (or Nai), the deceased. [I] come to thee, praised be thy beauties (read *nefruk*) ... praised be thy soul always (*r terui*), grant [me] to be in the nether world every day."

45. PLATE IX. Fig. 1. Limestone tablet, reused in the buildings of the forecourt of Tahutmes IV. "An offering which the king gives to Osiris Khentamenti, the Great God, Lord of the Necropolis, that he may give the funeral sacrifice of bread, beer, oxen, geese, linen cloths, vegetables, oil, thousands of all good and pure things, offerings, provisions, liquids, and all vegetables, which the heaven gives, the earth creates, and the Nile brings out of his source; [that he may give] the sweet wind of the north, and the drink from the whirlpool (?) of the river to the *ka* of the follower of his word on water and on land, in the foreign lands of the south and of the north. The fighter against the lands of the barbarians, who chastises every one who is revolting against the king in the land of the Retenu, filling the heart of the Good God, *Athu-usir*. He says, 'O, you living ones on earth, every priest, every scribe, every reciter who beholds this statue, the

image of my body upon earth, remember . . .'" The text ceasing here may have been continued on the lost part below, with perhaps the meaning "remember my name, and say the dedicatory formula of offerings." A rather similar address occurred at Koptos (see "Koptos" Pl. XVIII, 3, p. 17). The inscription of the lesser figure shows that the stele was dedicated to Athu-asar "by his beloved son, who makes his name to live, the stable-master of the Lord of the two lands *Min-mes*, renewing the life, the vassal of Osiris." The style of the work, which retains the traditions of the middle kingdom, gives the date as being early in the XVIIIth dynasty.

Fig. 2. The inscription from the back of the white bust of the queen (Pl. VI, 3, 4) refers in the first line to several dignities in the harim of some gods. These offices are denoted by the names of instruments, as is shown by the title *seshesky*[*t*] *en Mut*, "the player of the sistrum of Mut." (This title "shesh shyt" occurs among those of queen Titi, see De Rouge, Inscr. Hist. 249). Probably therefore the other titles are of similar nature. With *sesheshet* are sometimes named other instruments, *menat* and *sekhem* (Erman, Pap. Westcar, p. 61), though the latter reading is doubtful, but based on the demotic papyrus of Leiden I. 384 8132. The *men* at the close of the first line may have been *menyt*, and the title before Amen-Ra may have been the office composed with the sekhem. So I should translate—

"The . . . . playeress of Amen Ra, the sistrum playeress of Mut, the *menat* playeress of [Khonsu] . . . . Sais, the danceress (aheb[et]) of Horus . . . ." If this view of the reconstruction of the text is right, the queen had among other titles those of a lady of the *harim* of the Theban Triad. Unfortunately there is nothing in the inscription to reveal the name of the queen.

Fig. 3. This, and the following up to Fig. 20, depend upon Prof. Petrie's hand copies, as I have not seen the originals. Figs. 3 to 9 are inscriptions upon the bases of the colossal jackals which formed the avenue of approach to the temple of Amenhotep III. Fig. 3 reads ". . . . his inheritance, his kingdom [and] his throne, realising what he was doing in the land. His companion as king of the living. The two lands of Horus are under the direction ('plan' or 'design') of the Lord of the two lands Neb-maat-ra . . . . slaying the tribes of the Sati, the good God the brilliant image of Ra, shining like the sun's disc, Horus of the gods (or 'amongst the gods,' but this orthography of *nuter* would be very unusual at this time) with variegated feathers (?), for he has embraced the two lands with his wings, the son of Ra, Lord of the sword, Amenhotep prince of Thebes . . . ."

Fig. 4. "Great (?) in knowledge, there is nothing he does not know in heaven and earth, giving rule to the Spirits, who go forth at the sign of his eyes (? reading *semed n ártif*[*i*]) the king of Upper and Lower Egypt Neb-maat-[ra] . . . . The golden Horus, great by the sword, slaying the Sati. The southerners are coming to him on their bellies, the northerners on account of the power of his spirits. No land stays behind him (ignores him?). The son of Ra, Amenhotep. . . ."

Fig. 5. ". . . . great in vigour he has made [it] by his arms like the Lord of Thebes (Amen) . . . . slaying the Sati, not . . . ."

Fig. 6. "[Neb] maat [Ra], heir of Ra, beloved of Amen Ra, endowed with life."

Fig. 7. ". . . . fluid of life, firmness, purity (?), health, gladness."

Fig. 8. ". . . . in placing his fear amongst the hidden . . . . his terror is going through the lands, acting by his arms, making the two lands know the king of Upper and Lower Egypt, Lord of the sword, Neb-maat-ra . . . . slaying the Sati, overthrowing in all lands those who rebel against him, making foreign lands to be heaps of corpses, wounding (?) them, the terror of him is amongst all foreign lands, the son of Ra, Amen[hotep]."

Fig. 9. "[Neb] maat [Ra], image of Ra, beloved of Amen, endowed with life." "Amenhotep, prince of Thebes, beloved of Amen in eternity." "The fluid of life, firmness, purity, health, and gladness supports him like Ra every day in eternity." ". . . . son of Ra, beloved, endowed with life." ". . . . beloved of [Nehbet]-kau (?) like Ra."

Figs. 10-24. These graffiti are painted on the blocks of building stone, as masons' marks; they are not all comprehensible, and I only state what seems to me fairly clear. Figs. 11, 12, bear the name of a building of "the town" or "the south city" (Thebes); with *ankh nas* added, which elsewhere means the king's palace (Rec. Trav. xix. 89, 3). The first two signs may be the name of the building, perhaps of the temple of Tahutmes IV, where this was found. Fig. 13 reads *nefer renp.t*, "good years," which I noticed also on blocks of the temple at Deir El Babri. It may be the name of a man. Fig. 24 reads "position of filling," that is, the level of the sand filling of the foundation. It was written on a large pebble in the side of the foundation trench of Tausert's temple; a longer example of such inscription will appear amongst the ostraca of the Ramesseum.

Figs. 14 to 18, 21, and unnumbered piece 25. These are the most interesting of the graffiti, and the latter ones give the key to the others. They read "the great one of the mercenaries of the right hand Huy." We know from the papyrus of Tanis that there was a separation of troops into right (*unami*) and left (*semhi*) classes; and there it is very likely, as Horrack (Rev. Arch. 1862 ii, 268) and Brugsch (Aegyptologie 221) have observed, that a remembrance of this organization is implied by Herodotos when he states (II, 30) that Asmakh (or Askham) means "those that stand at the left hand of the king." This division into right and left appears also in the organization of the workmen of the Theban necropolis (e.g. Pap. Turin VII, 10), and is shown here by the title in the graffiti 14 to 18. It seems quite possible that the marks *unami*, right, and *semhi*, left, refer also to this military organization. In the fig. 20 the dates have been added "12th of 4th month of inundation" and 10 + x of the same; the black lines are written upside down to the red. To understand these graffiti we must remember that the necropolis of Thebes had several forts with garrisons, such are often named in business papers (Spiegelberg, *Arbeiter . . . . unter den Ramessiden*). These garrisons may well have been near the funerary temples, which we know had their troops. May then these marks "right" and "left" have indicated the place of the soldiers in the temple fortifications of the funerary temple of Merenptah, where they were found?

46. PLATE X, LIMESTONE STELE OF AMENHOTEP III. This sculpture has been intentionally defaced in all parts relating to the god Amen, and then subsequently restored by Sety I. At the top under the solar disc, with wings and uraei, is twice repeated "The god of Edfu (Horus) the great god, he gives life and purity." Between the uraei is the cartouche Neb-maat-ra. Below this the whole is divided into two scenes, each with a standing figure of "Amen-ra, lord of heaven, he gives all life and all health," who receives the offerings of the king. On the right side the incised inscription (restored) states "Restoring of the monument made by the son of Ra Sety Merenptah (Sety I) for his father Amen." The restored parts are the figures of Amen, the names of Amen, the cartouches of Amenhotep in the lower scenes, and the restoration inscription. The names of offerings before the king are probably original.

Right Side. Above the king is "The good god, lord of the two lands, Neb-maat-ra son of Ra, his beloved [Amenhotep, prince of Thebes] gifted with life like Ra." Below is "Offering of wine to Amen; may he give the gift of life."

Left Side. Above the king is "The Good God, lord of the two lands Neb-maat-ra son of Ra, of his body [Amenhotep, prince of Thebes] lord of the diadems, beloved of Ra." Below is "Giving truth to the lord of the gift of life (?)."

Lower Part. Right Side. Amenhotep triumphing in his chariot over the negroes. "The Good God [Lord of the foreigners] master of the sword, strong in binding them, who ruins the offspring of the vile Kush, guiding her chiefs as living prisoners by the power of his father Amen." There are some curious forms of signs (as *seger* and *sar*), and a brevity of orthography caused by the short space available.

Left Hand. Amenhotep triumphing in his chariot over the Syrians. "The Good God, the golden Horus, shining in truth, beautiful (?) like the sunrise, great in power, mighty in terror, firm of heart like he who is in Thebes (Amen) prostrating Nehereni with his victorious sword." If it be correct to give the sign of the horse the value *nefer*, which it has in Ptolemaic times, it would be of interest to find it thus early under Amenhotep III. We know that the germs of the Ptolemaic system are to be found long before their development, as in the writing of *mesdemt* in the Ebers papyrus (26, 18).

At the base ". . . . all foreign (?) lands, all men (*rekhyt*), all beings (*hnememet*), Nehreni, the vile Kush, the Upper and Lower Rethenu, are at the feet of this good god like Ra in eternity."

47. PLATES XI, XII, GREAT STELE OF AMENHOTEP III. At the top is the solar disc with wings and uraei, and on either side "The god of Edfu (Horus), the great god, lord of heaven." Between the uraei is the cartouche of Neb-maat-ra. Down the middle is "Restoring of the monument made by the king of Upper and Lower Egypt Men-maat-ra (Sety I) for his father Amen-ra king of all gods." • This proves the restoration by Sety after the erasures of Amen by Akhenaten. The restored parts are the figures and names of Amen, the whole of the first 21 lines, parts of 7 lines lower, and the names of Amen in the lowest 3 lines.

Right Hand. The king is standing, "Offering libation to Amen that he may give the gift of life." Above is "The Good God, lord of the two lands, Neb-maat-ra, Son of Ra, lord of the diadems, Amen-

THE INSCRIPTIONS.

hotep prince of Thebes. Great [by his] monuments, multiplying wonders, beloved by Amen, gifted with life." Over Amen is "I have given to thee all life and purity which is with me; I have given to thee all joy of heart which is with me, Amen Ra, lord of heaven."

Left Hand. The king is standing, "Offering wine to Amen, that he may give the gift of life." Above is "The Good God, Lord of the two lands, Neb-maat-ra: son of Ra, lord of the diadems, Amenhotep prince of Thebes; Image of Ra in the two lands, elected by himself, beloved of Amen, gifted with life." Over Amen is "I have given to thee all health which is in me; I have given to thee all vigour which is in me, Amen-Ra, prince of Thebes."

Below this is the long inscription here translated. As the text and commentary will soon be published in the *Recueil des Travaux*, only the simple translation is here given.

Introduction (Protocol, Lines 1-2).

|¹ Horus lives, the strong bull, brilliant with truth, the Unifier of both diadems, he who establishes the laws and calms both lands, the Golden-Horus, great in power, he who smites the Asiatics, the King of Upper and Lower Egypt, *Neb-maat-Ra*, the Son of the Sun *Amenhotep the Prince of Thebes*, beloved by Amon of Karnak, the chief god in Apet, gifted with life, whose heart rejoices, ruling both lands like Ra for ever |² the gracious god, the lord of joy of heart, he who watches over him who formed him, Amen, the king of the gods, he who makes his house great, he who makes his beauty content by doing what his *ka* loves. Thus his Majesty deigned to make very great monuments. Never occurred the like since the creation of the world.

The Temple of Amenhotep III upon the West Bank of Thebes (lines 3-10).

He made them |³ as his monument for his father Amen, the Lord of Karnak, making him a glorious house of the gods in the west of Thebes, a fortress of Eternity for eternity, of beautiful light-coloured sandstone, adorned (?) all over with gold; its floor is inlaid with silver, |⁴ all its doors with electron, large and very great, splendid for ever, and ornamented with this very great monument, with many royal statues of granite from Elephantine, of wonderful stones, and all kinds of precious |⁵ stones, finished as works of eternity. Its height shines up to the heaven, its rays fall into the faces as the Sun when he shines in the early morning. It (i.e., the temple) is provided with a Stele of the King, which is adorned with gold and many precious stones. The |⁶ masts are erected before it adorned with electron. It is like the horizon of the sky when Ra rises in it. Its sea is full like the high Nile, the Lord of the fish and the birds pure in . . . , its store-house is full of male and female slaves |⁷ of the children of the princes of all lands, which his Majesty has captured. Its store-houses contain beauties without number. Its magazines are surrounded by Syrian settlements, which are settled by the children of princes. Its cattle are |⁸ like the sand on the seashore, its *black* oxen are millions from South and North Egypt. (?) There his Majesty took counsel with himself (?) like Ptah, with skilful mind, like him in the Southwall, planning favours for his father Amen-ra king of the gods, since he made him |⁹ a very great Pylon before the face of Amon. His beautiful name, which his majesty had given, is "Amon has received his bark of the gods" [All this is] a resting-place of the Lord of the Gods at the valley festival at the procession of Amon in the West, when he looks upon the gods of the West, that he may reward |¹⁰ his Majesty with life and purity.

The Temple of Luxor (lines 10-16).

King Amenhotep III who awakens (?) contentment with the works of his father Amen Ra, the Lord of Karnak in the southern Apet, made of beautiful light-coloured sandstone, large and very great, |¹¹ increasing its beauty. Its walls are of electron, its floor of silver, all doors are adorned with . . . , its pylons reach to the sky, they join themselves with the stars. When men see them, |¹² they praise his Majesty. The King Neb-maat-Ra has appeased the heart of his father Amen of Karnak. To him every land is delivered, the Son of the sun Amenhotep, the ruler of Thebes, the splendour of Ra. . . . His majesty made another monument for his father Amen, he made him a castle (?) as an offering before the face of the southern Apet, |¹³ a place of recreation for my father at his beautiful festival. I have erected (*sdhd*) a great temple in its interior (?) (*khenu*), like Râ when he rises in the mountain of the Sun. It (i.e., the temple) is planted with all kinds of beautiful flowers. Nu is in its lake at all seasons |¹⁴. It has more wine than water, even as the Nile flows, the son of the lord of eternity (i.e., Osiris), who is rich, the seat which receives the tributes (?) of all lands, many gifts are brought before my father as tribute of all lands. He has given to me the lords of the lands of the south, |15 the inhabitants of the south, and those of the north. Each is joined to his neighbour. Their silver, their gold, their cattle, and all kinds of precious stones of their lands are in millions, hundreds of thousands, tens of thousands, and thousands. I have made it for my begetter in loyalty of heart (?) even as |16 he made me the Sun of the peoples of the Nine Bows (barbarians), the King of Upper and Lower Egypt, Nebmaat-ra, the image of the Sun, the Son of the Sun, Amenhotep the Prince of Thebes.

Temple of Karnak (lines 16–23).

I built another monument for my begetter Amon Ra in Karnak, who is firm on his throne, making him a great bark on the stream (with the name) "Amen Ra is in the User-hat," [even a] bark of new |17 cypress wood which his Majesty had felled (*shdd*) in the land of the god, and which has been drawn by the princes of all lands from the mountains of Retennu, very large and great. Never was anything like (it) done. Its body (?) is inlaid with silver, and adorned |18 all over with gold. The holy of holies (Naos) is of electron, and fills the whole earth. Its bows .... they unite the great *atf* crowns. Its snakes are on its sides. They are furnished with talismans behind themselves |19. The masts are firm opposite it (i.e., the holy of holies), adorned with electron, two great obelisks stand between them. It is altogether beautiful. The spirits of Pe exult before it, the spirits of Nechen praise it. The gods of the inundation of the north and south |20 embrace its beauty. Nu causes its bow to shine as the sun's disk shines in heaven, in order to make its beautiful procession at his (i.e., Amen's) festival of Apet, at its procession to the west of millions of millions of years. The King Amenhotep III |21 who watches over the glory of the King (lit. "to seek the brightness of the King"), has built another monument of Amen, making a very large pylon for him, before the face of Amen Ra of Karnak, adorned all over with gold. The shadow of the god is like a ram (?) set with real lapislazuli, adorned with gold, and with many precious stones. Never was the like made |22. Its floor is inlaid with silver, the gates opposite it stand firm. The steles are of lapislazuli, one on each side. Its pylons reach up to the sky, and the four pillars of the sky. Its flag-masts shine up to the sky |23 adorned

with electron. His majesty brought the gold for it from the land of Karoi, during his first victorious campaign, when he beat the wretched Ethiopian, the King of Upper and Lower Egypt, Neb maat Ra, the favourite of Ra, the Son of the Sun, Amen-hotep, the Prince of Thebes.

Temple of Soleb (lines 23–25).

I built other monuments for Amen. Its |24 like has not been made. I built thee thy house of millions of years on the estate (?) of Amon Ra of Karnak, Kha-em-maat, the sublime of electron, the place of repose of my father at all of his festivals, which is excellently made of beautiful light-coloured sandstone, ornamented all over with gold |25. The ornaments of its floor are of silver, all its gates of gold. Two great obelisks are erected, one on each side, between which my father rises. I am in his suite |26. I have sacrificed to him thousands of oxen .... thighs.

Speech of Amen: (lines 26–31).

Speech of Amen-ra king of the gods: My Son out of my body, my favourite Neb-maat-ra, my living image, created by my limbs, born of Mut the Lady of Ashru in Thebes, the Lady of the peoples of the Nine Bows, who bred thee |27 as the only lord of men. My heart is greatly rejoiced when I see thy beauties.

I do wonders for thy Majesty:
Thou becomest young again,
I have made thee the Sun of the Two Lands.

I turn my face towards the SOUTH,
(And) I do wonders |28 for thee:
(For) I make the lords of Ethiopia hasten to thee
With all their tributes on their backs.

I turn my face towards the NORTH,
(And) I do wonders for thee:
(For) I make the lands come from the ends of Asia
With all their tributes on their backs.
They dedicate themselves to thee |29 with their children.
They come (lit. "one comes") that thou mayest give them in return the breath of life.

I turn my face towards the WEST,
(And) I do wonders for thee:
(For) I make thee seize the Tahenu (Libyans),
They remember not,

They build this fortress in the name of |ᵃ thy
    ("my") Majesty
Surrounded by a great wall,
Which towers to the sky,
Settled with the children of the princes of the Nu-
    bian Troglodytes.

I turn my face towards the SUNRISE
(And) I do wonders for thee :
(For) I make the lands of Punt come to thee
With all kinds |ᵃ of pleasant spices of their lands,
To beg peace of thee,
And to breathe the breath, which thou givest,
King of Upper and Lower Egypt, Prince
Of the peoples of the Nine Bows, Lord of the two
    Lands,
Neb-maat-Ra, Son of the Sun, his favourite,
Amenhotep, Prince of Thebes ; content
Is the heart of the gods with his monuments—
He is gifted with life, stability,
Purity (?) and health. His heart
Rejoices like the Sun for ever.

48. PLATES XIII, XIV. GREAT STELE OF ME-
RENPTAH. This has been engraved on the rough
back of the stele of Amenhotep III., which was
removed from his temple, and placed back outward,
against the wall, in the forecourt of the temple of
Merenptah. Owing to the rough surface, and the
poor cutting, the readings in many places require
careful examination. For this, there have been used
(1) a hand copy by myself, taken at a disadvantage, as
it lay face downward ; (2) a paper squeeze, made by
Prof. Petrie ; (3) photographs of the stele, and of
squeezes of it, made by E. Brugsch Bey, on a larger
scale.

The scene at the top retains its original colouring
of yellow, red, and blue. Amen is shewn giving a
sword to the king, who is backed by Mut on one side
and by Khonsu on the other. Of the inscription a
copy was published in the Zeitschrift f. Ae. Sp. 1896
p. 1., with commentary by me. Hence only a plain
translation is given here.

THE TRIUMPHAL SONG OF MERENPTAH.

I. Protocol.

"In the year V., on the third day of the third
month of the period of inundation, under the Majesty
of Horus Ra, the strong bull, high in (?) truth, the
King of Upper and Lower Egypt Banera Meriamen,
son of Ra, *Merenptah-Hetephermaat* the increaser of
power, raising the victorious sword of Horus-Ra, the
strong bull, smiting the Nine Bows (foreigners) whose
name endures to all eternity."

II. MERENPTAH TRIUMPHATOR.

(a) Introduction.

"Report of his |ᵃ triumph in all lands, proclama-
tion to all lands together in order that may be known
the glory of the deeds of victory of King Merenptah,
the bull, the Lord of power,
Slaughtering his enemies,
Beautiful in the field of victory.
His attack is the sun,
Which frightens away the clouds that stand over
    Egypt.
He causes Egypt to see the sunbeams,
And overthrows the brazen mountain,
From the neck of the people;
He gives freedom to men who languish in imprison-
    ment,
He avenges Memphis upon its enemies,
He causes Ptah Totunen to rejoice over his foes,
He opens the gates of the City of Walls (Memphis)
    which were closed,
He causes the temples to receive again their meal
    offerings,
King Merenptah, he who makes firm the hearts of
    hundreds of thousands and of millions."

(b) The Defeat of Libya.

"At the sight of him the breath of life enters their
    nostrils,
The land of *Temehu* (Libyan tribe) stands open
    during his lifetime,
Eternal terror is laid in the heart of the *Masha-
    washa* (Libyan tribe)
He makes the tribe of the *Lebu* withdraw, having
    invaded Egypt.
Great fear of Egypt is in their hearts,
They were come their face in front (?)
They were turned backward (?)
Their legs did not stay firm, but fled,
Their archers threw their bows away,
Their runners were weary of (?) marching,
They unbound their skins
And threw them to the ground.
Their sacks (?) were taken and poured out (?)
The wretched conquered Prince of Libya fled,
Under the protection of the night,
Alone, without the plume on his head.

His feet failed (?)
His women were taken away before his face,
The provisions (?) of his store (?) were plundered,
He had no water skin for his sustenance,
His brothers plotted his murder,
His officers fought with one another,
Their camp was burned, made to ashes (?)
His whole property became a booty of the soldiers.
Arriving in his country he lamented,
Every one in his country was ashamed to receive him (?)
Punished prince, evil fate, 'feather'! (?)
Called him all the inhabitants of his city.
He is in the power of the gods, the Lords of Memphis.
The ruler of Egypt has cursed his name,
Mauroy is an abomination to Memphis,
With every descendant of his family forever ;
Banera-Meriamun pursues his children,
Merneptah-Hetephermaat is sent to him as a Fate,
He is become a proverb (?) for Libya.
The young men tell each other of his victories:
Since the time of Ra such has never happened to us! (?)
All old men tell to their sons :
Woe (?) over Libya !
One can no longer go pleasantly in the fields,
In a single day our walking has been made impossible,
In one year the *Tehenu* have been burned.
Sutech has turned his back to their princes,
Their settlements are wasted on account of him (?)
In those days one did not carry baskets, (?)
It was best to hide one's self,
One is safe (only) in the citadel (?).
The great ruler of Egypt,
Might and strength belong to him,
Who dares to fight, knowing his step!
A wretched and mad one is he who resists him.
He who transgresses his command,
Does not see the next day.
For Egypt is called since the reign of the gods,
The only daughter of Ra,
His son sitting upon the throne of *Shu*, the sun of Ra.
His heart is not forbearing (?) towards him,
Who outrages his inhabitants.
The eye of every god pursues him
Who abuses the . . . . .
It brings up the most distant foes—
Thus they speak (*sc.* the old men)

The seers of the stars (?)
Who know their meaning observing them say : (?)
A great wonder has come to pass in Egypt,
He has made him whom his hand reached,
A living prisoner.
The divine King triumphs (?) over his enemies before Ra.
Mauroy, the evil doer, is dashed down (?) by every god of Memphis.
He (*sc.* Ra) judges him in Heliopolis,
And the assembly of the gods declares him guilty of his crimes.

The Lord of the All says :
Give the sword of victory,
To my true-hearted, good and mild son Merenptah,
Who cares for Memphis (?)
And defends Heliopolis (?)
The cities closed shall be opened again,
He shall free many enchained in each district (?)
And give sacrifices to the temples (again).
He shall bring incense before the god again,
He shall bring back (?) again to the great their property,
And let the poor return (?) into their cities.—
The Lords of Heliopolis say to their son Merenptah :
May a long lifetime be his lot,
For he has defended the oppressed (?) of every foreign land.
Egypt shall be given to him as the heritage (?)
Of him, who has placed him (?)
As administrator for himself forever (?).
(For) his strength is its people.
Behold one is sitting safe in the time of the strong (?)
The breeze of life is on his arms (?)

The following is told :
Mauroy the wretched conquered prince of Libya came,
To attack the walls of the Prince (Memphis),
And [of] every (god) (?) who lets his son be brilliant upon his seat.
The King of Upper and Lower Egypt Merenptah.—
Ptah speaks to the prince of Libya :
All his crimes shall be collected,
And shall fall back upon his head ;
He shall be given into the hand of Merenptah,
That he may cause him to spit out,
What he has swallowed as a crocodile,
As the hastener brings up the hastening (?),
The Lord (*i.e.* Pharoah) shall seize him,

2 E

That he may know (?) his power.
Amon shall bind him with his hand,
And give him over to his *Ka* in Hermonthis,
King of Upper and Lower Egypt *Merenptah*.—

Great joy shall rule in *Kemet*,
Exultation shall rush forth from the cities of Tamera;
They shall tell of the victories,
Which Merenptah has won over the *Tehenu*, crying:
How dear is he the prince of the victory!
How great is the king among the gods!
How happy is he the Lord who commands!

One is talking:
Come far out upon the roads,
There is no fear in the heart of men,
The castles are abandoned ...
The wells opened (again),
The messengers return home (?)
The battlements lie calm in the sun (?)
Until their guards awake.
The soldiers lie in sleep
The *Nawt* and the *Tektína* are in the marsh they like,
The cattle are let on the pasture (?) (again).
No one fears (?) to go on the high Nile.
By night resounds not the cry: (?)
Stop! or come, come! (?) in the mouth of the people.
One goes with singing (?)
There is no more the lament of sighing man.
The villages are settled anew,
He who has tilled his crop will eat it."

(c) *The Defeat of the other Enemies of Egypt.*

"(For) Ra has turned himself again to Egypt;
He is born to avenge it,
The King of Upper and Lower Egypt Banera Meriamen, sun of Ra *Merenptah-Hetephermaat.*
The princes bend down, saying 'Hail!' (בשׁ)
Not one raises his head among the Nine Bows.
Devastated is Tehenu,
Kheta is quieted,
Seized is *the Kanaan* with every evil,
Led away is Askelon,
Taken is Gezer,
Yenoam is brought to nought,
The people of Israel is laid waste,—their crops are not,
Khor (Palestine) has become as a widow for Egypt,

All lands together—they are in peace.
Every one who roamed about
Is punished by King Merenptah, gifted with life, like the sun every day."

49. PLATE XV. STELE OF DUAUI-ER-NEHEH. This unfinished stele of limestone was found in the ruins of the temple of Amenhotep II. The following is the transliteration:

Top, Left Hand. Ari pátiu háti semer áa n merut. Mer per uer Duáui-er-neheh, átef Benáa, mutef Mesutá.

Top, Right Hand. Uden ákhet neb nefret uábet n mer per [*uer Duáui-er-neheh*].

Long Inscription. Ari pátiu háti . . . ti báti teken em setni uá res tep (?) *her neb em bek her hehi áakhut en nebf sethen n setni her menkh ábf er árt mekru thesutf ; mer per uer Duáui-er-neheh maá-kheru. Hak árf em hetep dá setni ákhet neb nefret nezmet sekhep uáb her heteptek shemst*(u)*k án kauk er sutk uábet r setk ent Ra-kreret em hetep em hetep kher neter áa, mer per uer Duáui-er-neheh maá-kheru. Ezdef kher remthet unenyu esdá enthen khepret ná her ártná em shems áty shemsná su her mu her ta khet khaset resit mehtit en áu sepá em setp-sa árná zedet-nef menkh*(a) *sekhent kuá er mátá neb erdákuá em hát semeruf ááná áa er net neheh árná mereret remthet heseset enteru sená ta em sáh neb hesyu en neter nefer káhná tet her rensen áru ná hetep dá setni má nu árná tep ta ánuk sáh en ártnef sed nefret uhem mereret nefer pu árt her áry*(u)*t.*

Translation. "The hereditary prince, the most beloved friend, the great major-domo Duaui-er-neheh. His father Benaa. His mother Mesut. Offering of all good and pure things for the [great] major-domo [Duaui-er-neheh.]

|¹ The hereditary prince, the treasurer of the king of Upper and Lower Egypt, who approaches the king of Upper Egypt, the only one who watches while all else are tired of seeking the glory of his Lord, |ᵇ whom the king has raised up by reason of the ability of his heart to care for his levy(?), the great major-domo Duaui-er-neheh, the deceased. Thou art going down |ᵇ with the royal offering, consisting of all good and sweet things, the sacred linen (?; is brought to thy sacrifices, thou art followed by thy *kas* to thy pure places, to thy places of Ra-kreret, |ᵇ in peace, in peace, with the great god, the great major-domo Duaui-er-neheh, the deceased. He speaks to the men who are living : I tell you what happened |ᵇ to me when I was follower of the king. I followed him by water and by land, through the countries both south and north. There

THE INSCRIPTIONS.

was no reproach [⁶ against me coming to the palace. I did what he said in an excellent manner (?). I was raised above every equal, and was put at the head of his friends. [Now], I am coming ⁷ to the city of eternity (the other world). I have done what mankind loves, and the gods praise. I am buried like every noble distinguished by the Good God. Stretch forth to me (your) hand in their name, make [⁸ for me the *hetep da setni* (recital of royal offering) according to what I did upon earth. I am a noble by what he made me, telling those things that are good, repeating those things that are dear, (for) it is good to reward a man according to his works."

l. 2. "levy," see Griffith, Kahun papyri i. 2.

l. 3. *Uáb* may be the same as the word determined by cloth in "Tomb of Paheri" (IX. 4).

l. 3. Ra-kreret is especially the necropolis of Siut.

50. PLATE XVI. The foundation deposits give the two names of the wife of Siptah called Te-usret-sotpet-ne-Mut and Sit-Ra-meri[t]-Amen, of whom scarabs are also known. There are some other instances of the article being merely written as *t* in the XIXth dynasty: see in Brit. Mus., stele 132, and palette 12,778.

PLATE XVIII. No. XIV. reads "may Ra and Amen open a good year." No. 7., "firm (steady) every year." No. 13., "chief treasurer of the whole land, chief Bay."

PLATE XIX. Among the vases of the foundation deposits of Tausert and Siptah there are two complete copies of a text, 6 and 10, with a piece 9, and perhaps other pieces, 7 and 8: it is remarkable for the very cursive handwriting, especially in the form of the article. It reads:—

"Year IV. Wine of the third day of the garden in the Lake of the Whole Land, which is in . . . on the western bank, by the chief vintner Pra-hotpe, who is under the land steward Pi-besa."

The other complete piece, No. 5, reads:

"Year III. Wine of the third day of the garden of the temple of Sety Merenptah (Sety II) in the house of Amen, which is the farm (?) of Tum, by the chief vintner . . . Anana." For this reading of the "third day," see the full transcription which will appear in the volume on the Ostraca of the Ramesseum.

No. 4 may be restored thus:—

[Year *x*, wine of the] "garden of the house of Sety Merenptah (Sety II), in the house of Amen, [by the chief] vintner Pa-mer-shunet."

No. 3 again mentions "the garden of the house of Sety II."

No. 1 is part of an inscription naming the wine of the garden of the "temple of millions of years," of a place (perhaps "the water of Amen") "on the west of Thebes."

No. 2 is one of the most important fragments, reading: "[Year *x*] wine of the 21st day . . . queen of Upper and Lower Egypt, Sit-ra-merit-Amen. . . ." Though it is not clear in what connection the name of queen Tausert occurs here, yet this gives the full and clear reading of the name. The queen here has the title of the king *setni ebyoti*, whose feminine form did not exist. (See *Sethe Untersuchungen,* i, 27).

PLATE XX. Here are also some other fragments of wine jars, but not from foundation deposits. No. 8 reads:—

"[Year *x*, wine] of the temple of millions of [years . . . in the house of] Amen, which is in the north of the property of Ramessu II . . . by the chief vintner . . . ."

No. 12. " . . . the garden of Merenptah Hetep-her-maat . . . Puah."

No. 13. " . . . wine of the fourth day of the . . . west by Puah."

No. 10. " . . . wine . . . by the vintner (?) Su-ne-[ra ?]"

No. 11 names a "prophet Sety," who is also known by another piece found in the excavations.

Of the other fragments, No. 1 seems, so far as can be seen, to be a piece of a business letter; all that is legible is "The prince is standing over the work, one is . . . his *áu* let . . . "

No. 2 reads: "The men of the farm (?, *qáḥt*) who one will

"arrest (?) (*áṭau ?*)

"[Pa] ur, his mother Ḥenut

" . . . tny, his mother Atef-res

" . . . , his mother Ḥent-Ty (?)

" . . . . . . son of Tent-nub."

No. 3. In this fragment, only the beginning of the name of Amenhotep II is clear.

No. 4. A razor and a pair of sandals; perhaps, as Prof. Petrie suggests very ingeniously, a bill of exchange.

No. 7. Duplicate of the beginning of the "Nile hymn" (Pap. Sall. II, ii, 6–7 = Anast VII, vii, 7–8). The variant *shems* for *seshm* is to be noted.

No. 6. "Third month of the sowing season, 13th day of delivering (?) the bread to the vinedressers by Hui and Pay. Prs (?) cake, 100 deben daily. Received from him in the third month of the sowing season, at the temple of Tahutmes III (*sic*) life, health

... " This is an account of provisions for the vinedressers: in ancient times the Theban western canal was rich in vineyards.

No. 5. The group *bek sed* is written twice with a thick reed, as a pupil's exercise.

[51. I should add that Dr. Spiegelberg has very kindly used here the transliteration with which English readers are perhaps most familiar; but this is without any prejudice to his personal preference for a different method.

I may add here some considerations on the mention of the name Israel in the inscription of Merenptah. This subject was opened in an article on "Egypt and Israel" which I published in the "Contemporary Review," May, 1896. The principal considerations are on the five different views that may be taken about the presence of "people of Israel" in wars of Merenptah.

(*a*) It might be taken to refer to the oppression of the Biblical Israelites in Egypt. As Merenptah is usually thought to be the Pharaoh of the Exodus, Israel being spoiled so that it had no seed might be taken as a reference to the slaughter of the male children. But on the contrary this statement is put between the naming of Yenuamu (or Yanuh near Tyre), and of Khal or Palestine. Hence it should refer to spoiling some Israelites in Palestine.

(*b*) It might be supposed to refer to the Biblical Israelites in Palestine after the Exodus. But as there is no trace of any Egyptian invasion of Palestine in the various wars and turmoils recorded in the book of Judges, we can hardly refer this to the Israelite history that we know. As moreover there is no trace of the campaigns of Ramessu III in the book of Judges, the Biblical Israelites can hardly have been in Palestine even as late as that. I have shown in the Proceedings of the Society of Biblical Archæology, xviii, 243 ; Dec. 1896; how the lists of generations, and the division of the history of Judges into three series of different regions, agree to the Israelites not entering Palestine till after the last campaign of Ramessu III.

(*c*) It is very possible that some portion of "the people of Israel" remained in Palestine when the others went into Egypt. And this might be the people attacked by Merenptah. Such a view seems to me to be perhaps less unlikely than any other.

(*d*) Some Israelites may have gone back to Palestine directly the famine was over in Canaan. That they readily might travel there is shewn by the burial of Jacob at Machpelah (Gen. i. 13); and there is absolutely no evidence that they all remained in Egypt until the Exodus. A continuity of tradition about the family sepulchres is shewn by the recognition of the cave at Machpelah, and of the burial place at Shechem. And this implies that some members of the clan continuously lived in the country.

(*e*) Another possibility is that immediately after the Exodus some Israelites may have made their way into Palestine, as they prospected in the land, wishing to occupy it, and even defeated the Canaanites in the south (Num. xxi, 3) in what appears to be another version of the conflict soon after the Exodus (Num. xiv. 45).

Neither the hypothesis *a* nor *b* seem likely, when we look at the order of the inscription here, and the complete silence about Egyptian invasions in Judges. If we then resort to one of the hypotheses of a divided body of Israelites, the hypothesis *a* seems more probable than the others, as these "people of Israel" seem to have been in the north of Palestine, and are less likely therefore to have gone into Egypt or to have come out again.

It may be noted that a duplicate of this inscription existed at Karnak, of which Duemichen has published the remaining fragment in *Historische Inschriften* 1 c. His line 1 ends at near the end of line 11 here; 2 at mid line 12; 3 mid line 13; 4 early in line 14; 5 late in line 14; and so on, evidently omitting a line between 8 and 9, until his last line, 19, ends at one third along line 27 here. There were therefore 34 lines in the Karnak copy, 12 lost at the beginning, 20 of which the ends remain (one omitted by D.) and 2 lost at the end. One difference may be noted in the texts, the present version attributes the divine speech to Ptah (l. 19), while the Karnak version names Amen (l. 10). W. M. F. PETRIE.]

CHAPTER X.

SHELLS USED BY THE EGYPTIANS.

52. In earlier excavations at Koptos, Ballas, and Naqada, many specimens of shells were collected ; and these have now been identified by the care of Mr. Edgar A. Smith of the British Museum (Natural History). To this list I have added those names which are given by M. de Morgan as belonging to the remains of the New Race, in "Recherches sur les Origines de l'Egypte," pp. 145-6. In the column of region, R.S. = Red Sea and Indian Ocean ; M. =

Mediterranean; N. = Nile; E. = Egypt (land). In the column of locality, B. = Ballas, with the number of the tomb; N. = Naqada, with the tomb number; Z. = Zowaydeh; the numbers in loops are the number of examples. K. = Koptos, and such are not dated. All of the others are of the New Race period.

Ætheria Cailliaudi	*Férus.*	N.	(De Morgan.)
,, elliptica	*Lamk.*	N.	B. 65; B. 760; K.
Arca (Anadara) antiquata	*Linn.*	R.S.	K. (2).
Cadium pomum	*Linn.*	R.S.	(De Morgan.)
Cardium edule	*Linn.*	M.	B. 519 (6).
Cassis nodulosa var.	*Gmel.*	R.S.	B. 207.
Cleopatra bulimoides	*Oliv.*	N.	B. 672 (78); B. 590 (De Morgan).
Columbella ligula	*Récl.*	R.S.	N. 1234 (10).
Conus ceylanensis	*Hwass.*	R.S.	Z. 23 (4), K.
,, pusillus	*Chemn.*	R.S.	(De Morgan).
,, striatus	*Linn.*	R.S.	N. 1503.
,, tessellatus	*Born.*	R.S.	K.
,, textile var.	*Linn.*	R.S.	B.; N. 1684; South Town; K.
,, sp.		R.S.	B. 655 (4).
Cypraea annulus	*Linn.*	R.S.	K.
,, arabica	*Linn.*	R.S.	K.
,, ,, (reticulata)		R.S.	(De Morgan.)
,, carneola	*Linn.*	R.S.	B.
,, caurica	*Linn.*	R.S.	B.?
,, erosa	*Linn.*	R.S.	B.
,, pantherina	*Solan.*	R.S.	N. South Town (2).
Engina mendicaria	*Lamk.*	R.S.	K. (3).
Helix desertorum	*Forsk.*	E.	N. 1615 (2).
,, melanostoma	*Drap.?*	E.	K.
Heterocentrotus mammilatus (spine)		..	K. (De Morgan)
Limnea stagnalis var.		N.	
Lotorium tritonis	*Linn.*	R.S.	K.
Mamilla maura	*Lamk.?*	R.S.	B.
Mitra maculosa	*Reeve*	R.S.	B. (22).
,, (strigatella) literata	*Lamk.*	R.S.	K.
Nerita crassilabrum	*Smith?*	R.S.	N. 1429.
,, polita	*Linn.*	R.S.	K. (2); B. (2); (De Morgan).
,, sp.		R.S.	B. 28 (14); B. 580; B. 655 (7); N. 1567.
Oliva sp.		R.S.	N. 1567; K.
Ositinus sp.		..	B. 580.
Ovula ovum	*Linn.*		B. 519 (2).
Pectunculus violacescens	*Lamk.*	M.	B. 519 (40).
,, sp.		M.	N. 1684.
Polinices mamilla	*Linn.*	R.S.	B. 572; K.
Pterocera bryonia	*Gmel.*	R.S.	K. (3).
Purpura tuberculata	*Blain.*	R.S.	(De Morgan.)
Rostellaria curvirostris	*Lamk.*	R.S.	K.
Sistrum anaxares	*Ducl.*	R.S.	(De Morgan.)
Spatha Cailliaudi		N.	(De Morgan.)
,, rubens	*Lamk.*	N.	B. 456, 471, 568.
,, sp.		N.	K.
Strombus fasciatus	*Born.*	R.S.	(De Morgan.)
,, tricornis	*Lamk.*	R.S.	K. (young).
Terebra caerulescens	*Lamk.*	R.S.	N. 1567.
,, consobrina	*Desh.*	R.S.	N. 1567; K.
,, maculata	*Linn.*	R.S.	K. (5).
Turbo sp. ? (opercula)		R.S.	K. (2).
Unio Aegyptiacus	*Caill.*	N.	B. 191, 760, 767. (De Morgan.)
,, dembese	*Reeve*	N.	B. 522.
,, teretiusculus	*Phil.*	N.	(De Morgan.)
Vivipara unicolor	*Oliv.*	N.	B. 672 (47); (De Morgan).

(32)

INDEX.

	PAGE		PAGE		PAGE
Aahmes, or stele	5	Ashu-asir, stele of	4, 21	Foundation deposits, Amenhotep II	5
Akhenaten, erasures by	4, 10, 11	Avenue of couchant jackals	10	Foundation deposits, Merenptah	13
Altars of temples	12	Azimuths of temples	20	
Amen, erasure of	10, 11			Foundation deposits, Tausert, 14, 15
Amenemhat, stele of	4, 20	Bakt, stele of	4, 20	„ „ Siptah, 16, 17
Amenhotep II, dated jar of	5	Bay, chancellor	16	„ „ inscriptions	29
„ scarab of	3, 21	Beads, rough carnelian	17	
„ temple of	3, 4–6	Benna, on stele	5	Foundation trenches, 11, 13, 16, 22
„ statue of	5	... pottery	6	
„ statuette of	5, 21	Brace cranks (?)	19	
„ length of reign	5	Brickwork arching on stone architraves	12	Gezer	28
„ altar in ruins	4			Gravels of high Nile	11
Amenhotep III, restores chapel of Uazmes	3, 11	Brickwork store chambers of Merenptah	12	Haworth, Mr. Jesse	2
Amenhotep III, ring of	3	Brickwork tunnels of Rameses	1	Helmet, bronze	18
„ re-works temple of Amenhotep II 4, 6, 9, 11		Bronze statuette of a queen	6	Hieroglyphs, mode of writing	5
Amenhotep III, temple of, reserved	9	„ helmet and bowl 18, 19		Huy	23
Amenhotep III, temple W. of Thebes	24	Capital of column	13	Ingot model	15
Amenhotep III, temple of Luxor	24	Centre-bits, iron	19	Iron tools	18, 19
		Chalybes, iron-workers	19	Israel inscription	2, 28, 30
Amenhotep III, temple of Karnak	25	Chisels, iron	19	Jackals, couchant, avenue of	9
		Colonnade, triple	8	Jar with date of Amenhotep III	5
Amenhotep III, temple of Soleb	25	Cubit lengths	7, 11, 13	Kanaan	28
		Dealers of Thebes	2	Kennard, Mr. Martyn	2
Amenhotep III, sculptures of 9–11, 20, 23–28		Dehnet, goddess	20	Kheta	28
Amenhotep III, inscriptions of 21–28		Deir el Bahri, plan of 7, 8, 12		Khonsuardus, tomb of	18
		Doorway south of temples	8	Khor (Palestine)	28
Amenhotep IV, figure of	10	Drawing trials	4, 17	
Anni, on stele	5	... ... stele of	5, 28	Lateran obelisk	5
... ...	12	Dusemnb, altar of	17, 21	Lebu	26
Asar-hapi invoked	18			Level of water	11
Ash, Syrian goddess	9, 21	Excavations, success in	1	Libyans, figures of	6
Asiexion	28			„ defeat of	26–28
Assyrian helmet and tools 18, 19		File, iron	19	
Aten-temple seal	6, 21	Foundation deposits, Uazmes	3	Magnetic variation	20
		„ „ early	4	Maket tomb, Kahun	8

INDEX.

	PAGE
Manetho vindicated	5
Mashawasha	26
Merenptah destroys temple of Amenhotep III, 9; bricks used by, 11; temple of, 11–13; black granite stele of, 13; statues of, 13	
Mesut, on stele	5
Min-mes, stele of	4, 22
Model tools	5, 15, 16
Mud beds, ancient	11, 18
Murray, Miss, publishes hieroglyphs	5
Nebmes, on stele	5
Nefer-renpit, on stele	5
Nefret, on stele	5
Nefret-ari, on stele	20
Nehi, ushabti of	4, 21
Nen, on stele	20
Nile-mud, beds of	11, 18
Osiride figures	4, 5
Osiride pillars	11, 12
Ostraka	29
Panehesi, vine-dresser	5, 21
Pashed, steles of	3
Pekh-ar-Khonsu	18
Pendehnet, on stele	20
Pendua, on stele	20
Pen-rannut, stele of	13, 21
Plan of temples	19, 20
Plummet of stone	9
Pottery, drawings on	17
„ spotted	6
„ blue	6
„ of Tahutmes IV	8
Psamtek III	7
„ tomb of	18
Ptah-hes, stele of	13, 21
Qazauadana	21
Quarry marks	9, 22
Queen, bronze statuette of	6

	PAGE
Queen, unknown, chapel of	6
„ „ statue of	22
Quibell, Mr., at the Ramesseum	1
Ra, priest of Tahutmes III, 4, 5, 20	
Ra, on stele	5
Ramesseum, living in	1
Ramessu IV, drawing of	17
Rasp, iron	19
Red outlines of drawing	5
Results from wide clearances	1
„ of past excavations	2
Rosettes for dress	5
Ruti, on stele	5
Sandals and razor marked on jar	9
Saws, iron	19
Scarp, in gravels	13, 18
Scoop cutter, iron	19
Sensenb, on stele	5
Sesh, royal scribe	6, 21
Sety I, restorations by	10, 11, 23
Sety II, garden of	29
Shells used by Egyptians	30
Sickle, iron	19
Siptah, relation to Tausert	15
„ temple of	16, 17
Sistrum, blue glazed	9
Sitamen, temple of	3, 6, 9, 11
Sphinxes of Amenhotep III	10
Spiegelberg, Dr. W.	2, 20, 30
Stamp for wine jars	7, 21
Statues of Amenhotep II, 5; of Tahutmes IV, 9; of Amenhotep III, 10; of Merenptah, 13	
Statuettes of wood	4, 5
Steles of Athu-asir, 4; of Tahutmes IV, 9, 20; of Amenhotep III, limestone, 10, 23; black granite, 10, 11, 23; of Merenptah, 13, 26; Pen-rannut, 13, 21	

	PAGE
Taharqa, pylon of	10
Tahutmes I, cartouche of	4, 20
„ ushabti of (?), 4, 5, 21	
„ III, priest of	4, 5, 20
„ IV, temple of	3, 7–9
„ portraits of	9
Takushet, statue	6
Tank of temple	12
Tas-nub	17, 21
Tausert, temple of	13–16, 23
„ cartouches of	15, 29
„ history of	15
Tehenu	27, 28
Temehu	26
Temples (see kings' names).	
„ plan of	19, 20
Tombs, fragments of, 3, 20; under temple of Tahutmes IV, 7, 8; of XXIInd dynasty, 4; of XXIIIrd dynasty, 18	
Trenches of foundations, 11, 13, 16	
Trial pieces of drawings	4
Troops, organization of	23
Tua, statue of	6
Tubes of glazed pottery	6
Uazmes, chapel of	3
User-aah, on stele	5
Ushabti of Nehi	4, 21
White queen, chapel of	6
„ „ bust of	22
Wine-jar ostraka	29
Work, expected and unexpected	1
Work, site of	1
Workmen from Koptos	2
„ Theban	2
Writing of hieroglyphs on stele	5
Yenoam	28

THEBES. INSCRIPTIONS OF XVIII. DYNASTY.

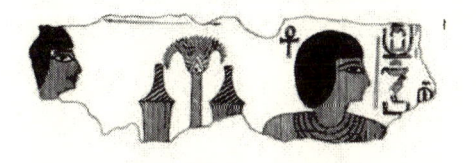

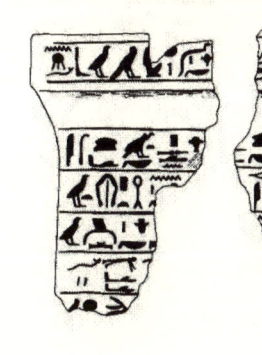

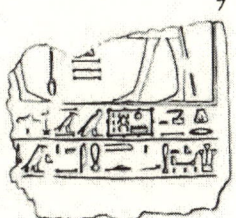

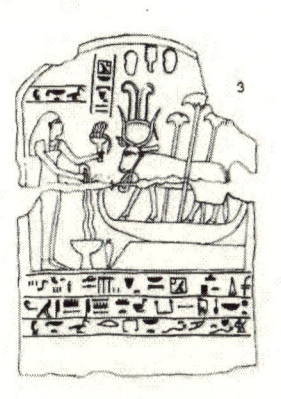

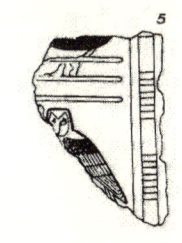

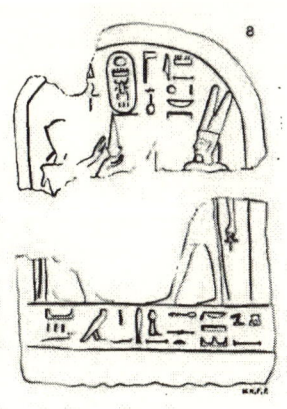

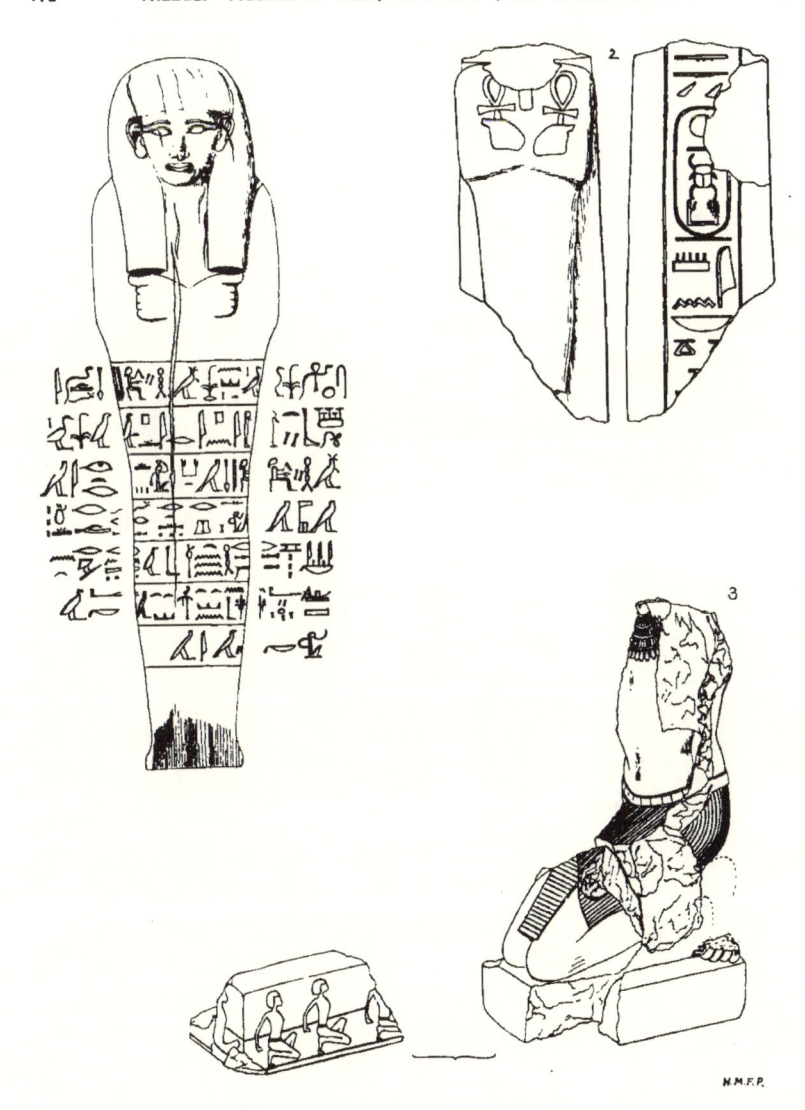

1:2 THEBES. FIGURES OF NEHI, TAHUTMES I, AND AMENHOTEP II. II.

1:2   THEBES. FOUNDATION DEPOSITS, &c. XVIII–XIX DYNASTY.   III.

AMENHOTEP II & SITAMEN.

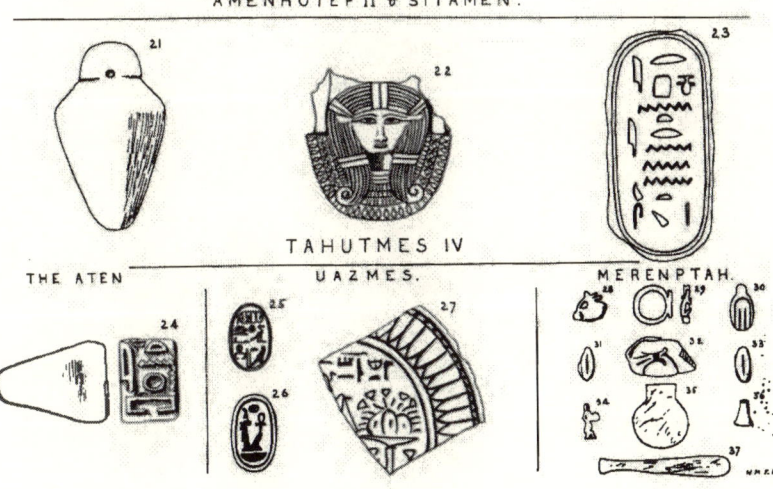

THE ATEN   TAHUTMES IV   MERENPTAH.
           UAZMES.

1:2　　THEBES. POTTERY OF FOUNDATION DEPOSIT, XVIIIth DYN.?　　IV.

THEBES. POTTERY OF FOUNDATION DEPOSIT, AMENHOTEP II.

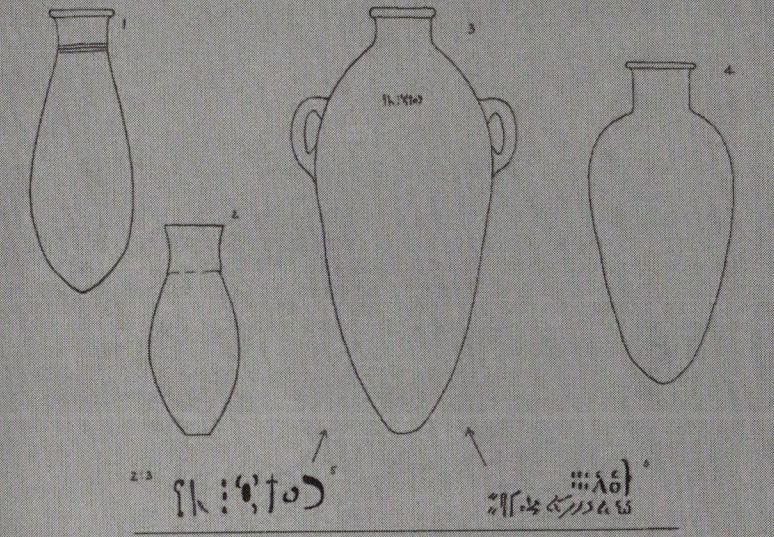

THEBES. POTTERY OF AMENHOTEP II.

POTTERY OF AMENHOTEP II.? OR III.

THEBES. PORTRAITS OF KINGS, &c. VI.

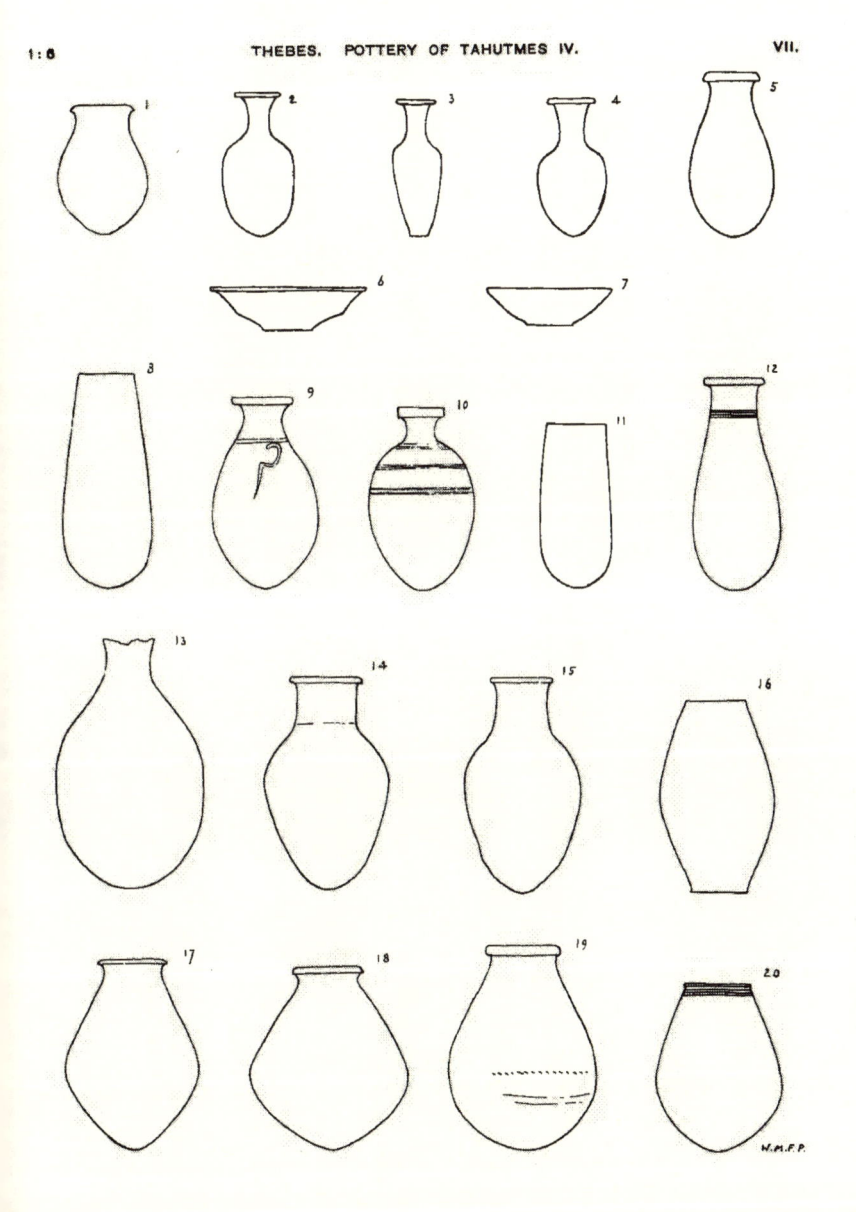

1:6 THEBES. POTTERY OF TAHUTMES IV. VII.

1:2   THEBES.   TABLETS OF XVIII–XIX DYNASTIES.   VIII.

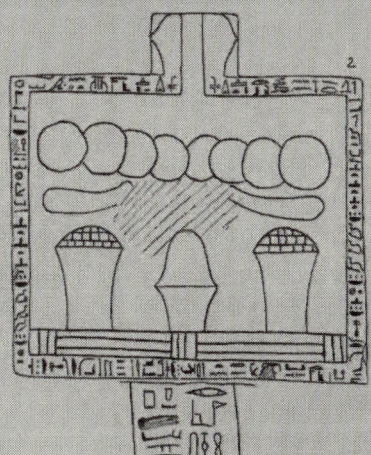

THEBES. INSCRIPTIONS OF XVIII.–XIX. DYN. IX.

THEBES. LIMESTONE STELE OF AMENHOTEP III. PL. X.

THEBES. BLACK GRANITE STELE OF AMENHOTEP III. PL. XI.

THEBES. STELE OF AMENHOTEP III.

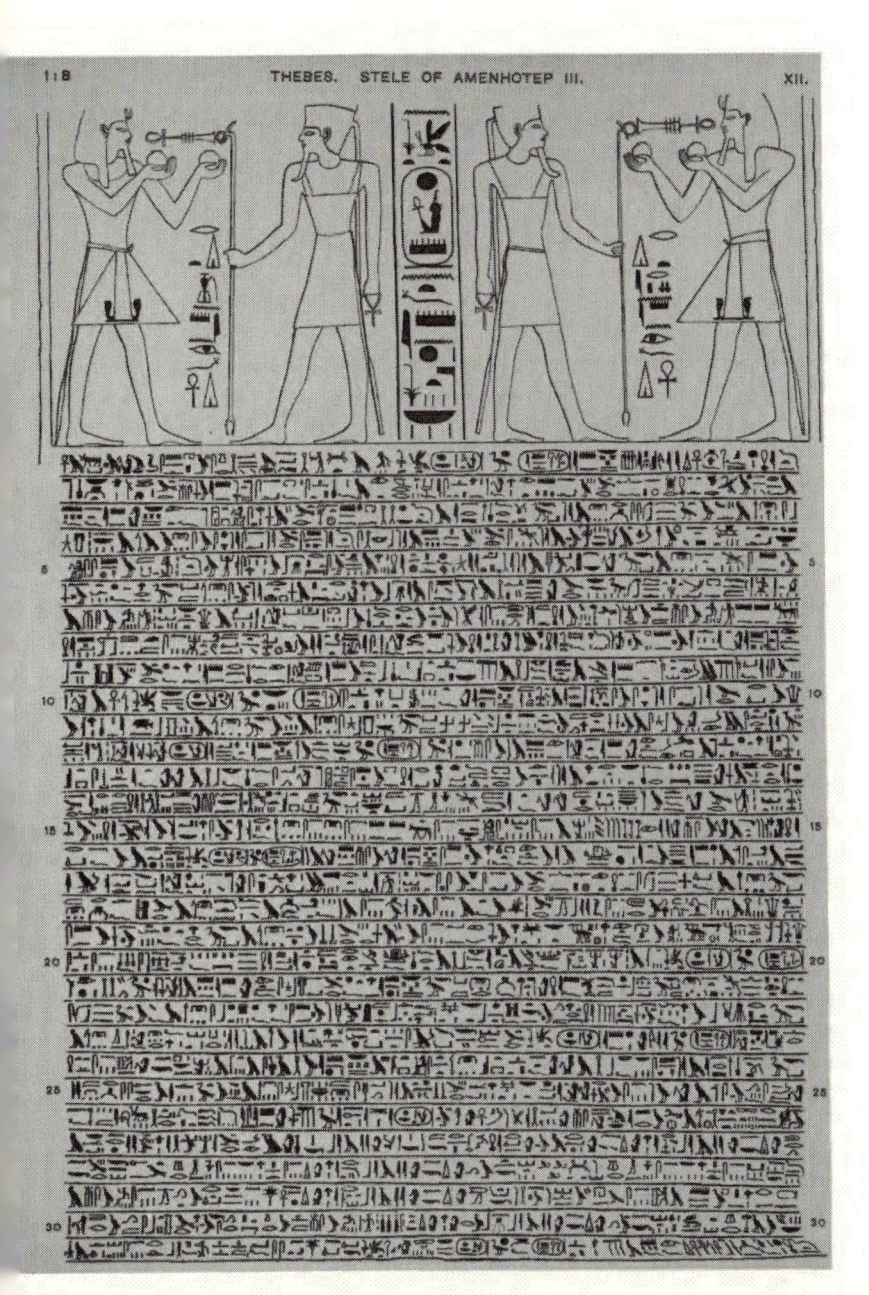

THEBES. BLACK GRANITE STELE OF MERENPTAH. PL. XIII.

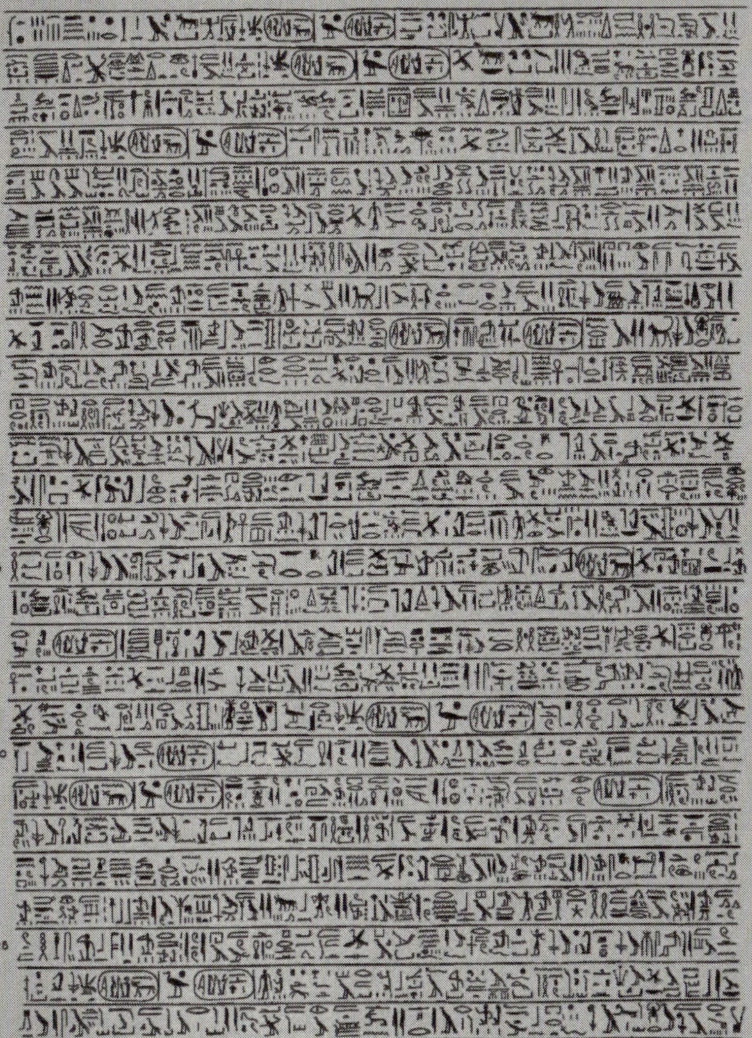

THEBES. OUTLINED STELE OF DUI-ER-NEHEH. PL. XV.

THEBES. FOUNDATION DEPOSITS OF TAUSERT. XVI.

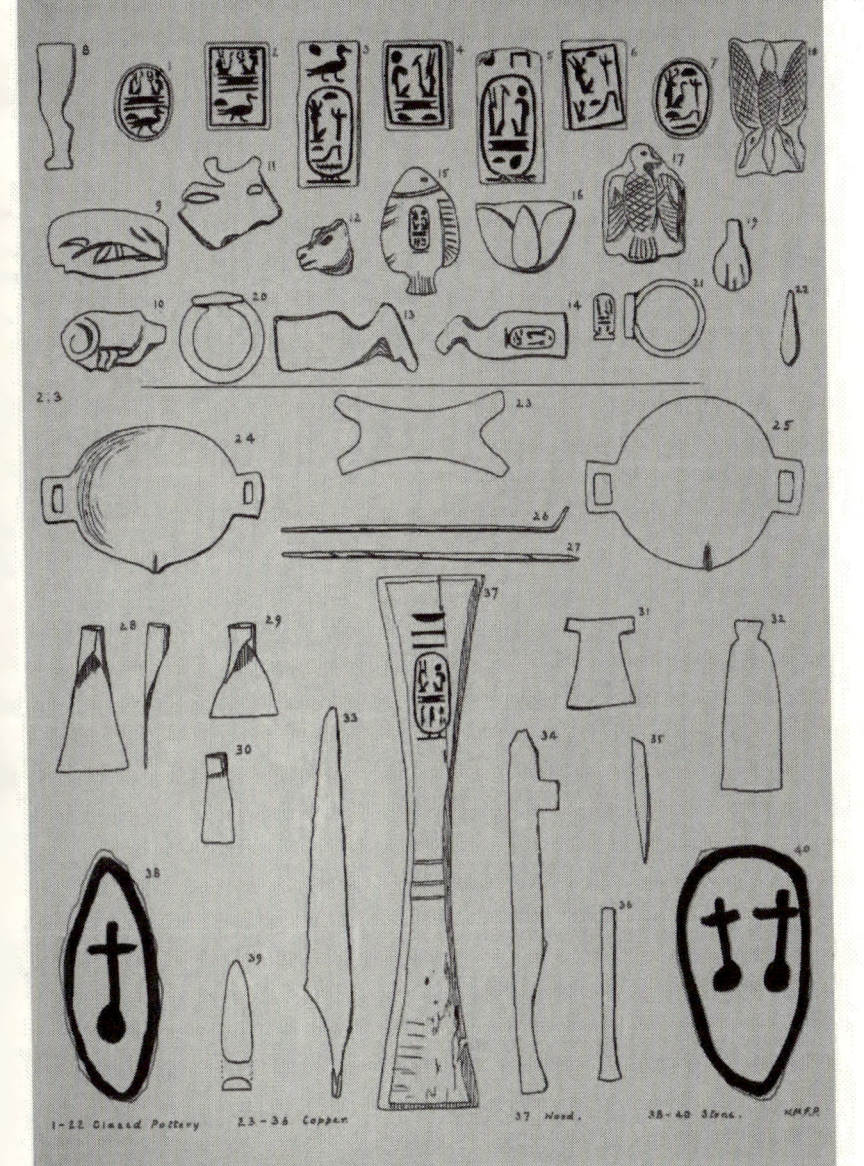

1-22 Glazed Pottery. 23-36 Copper. 37 Wood. 38-40 Stone.

THEBES. FOUNDATION DEPOSITS OF SIPTAH. XVIII.

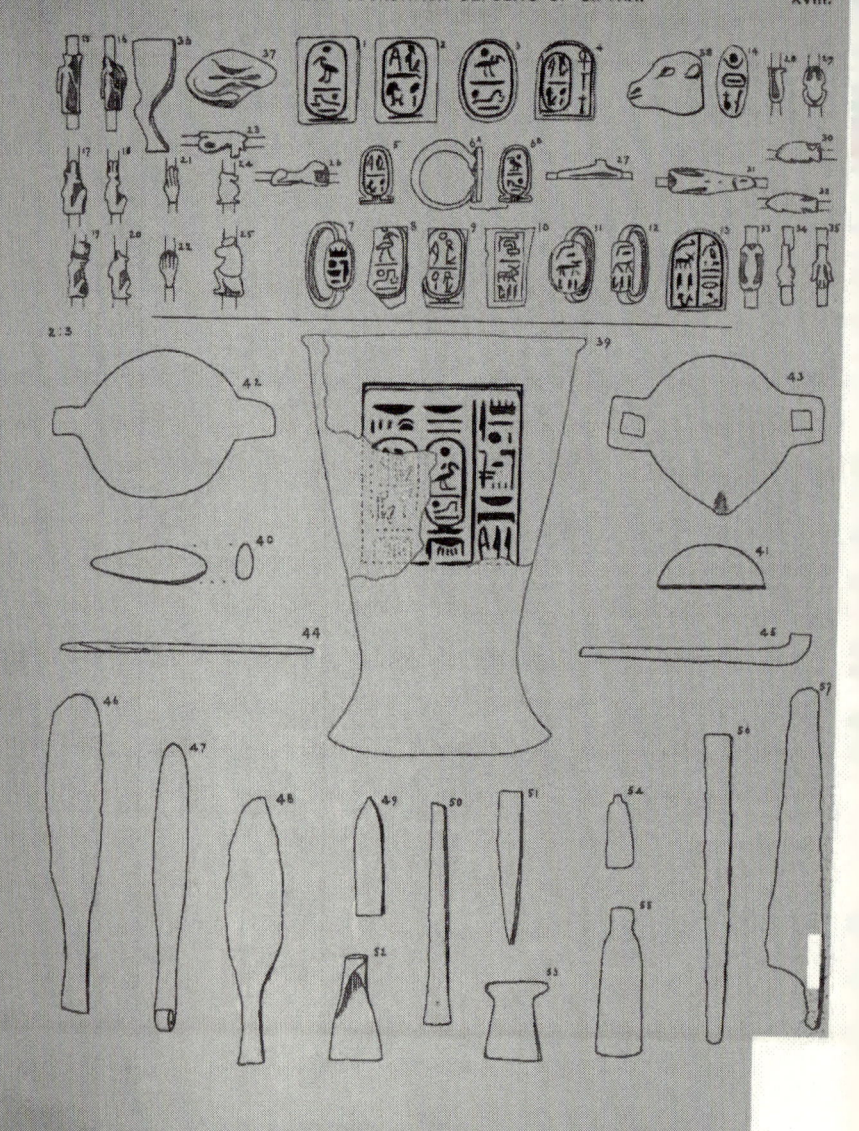

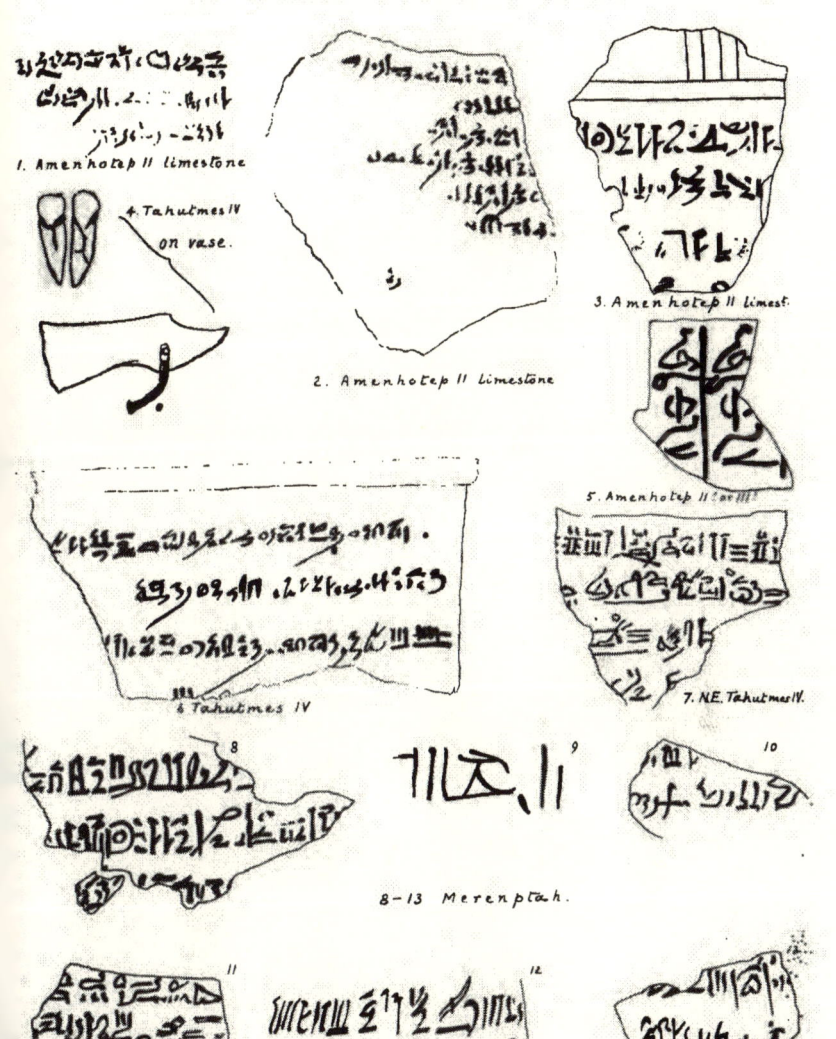

THEBES. INSCRIPTIONS, AMENHOTEP II. TO MERENPTAH.

1. Amenhotep II limestone
2. Amenhotep II limestone
3. Amenhotep II limest.
4. Tahutmes IV on vase.
5. Amenhotep II or III
6. Tahutmes IV
7. N.E. Tahutmes IV.
8–13 Merenptah.

THEBES. ASSYRIAN HELMET, BOWL, AND TOOLS. PL. XXI.

1:4000 THEBES. GENERAL PLAN OF TEMPLES. XXII.

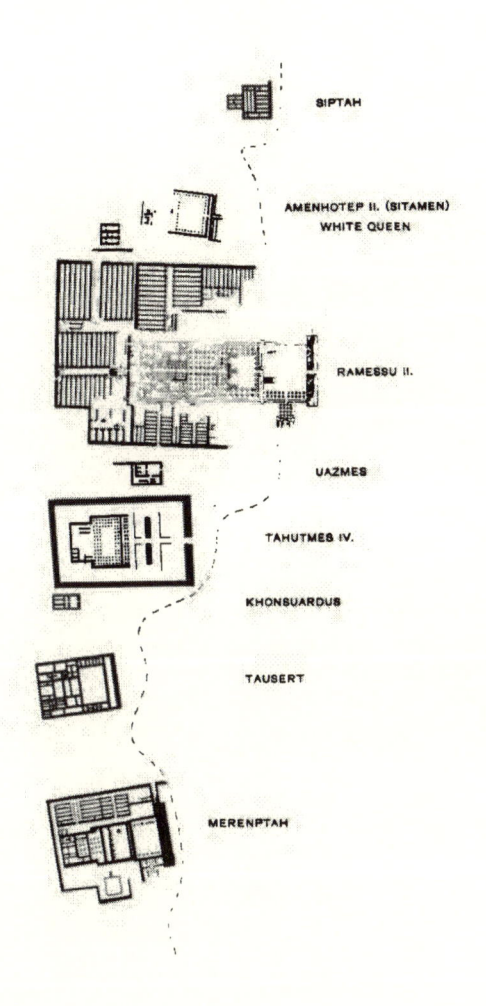

SIPTAH

AMENHOTEP II. (SITAMEN)
WHITE QUEEN

RAMESSU II.

UAZMES

TAHUTMES IV.

KHONSUARDUS

TAUSERT

MERENPTAH

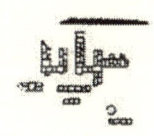

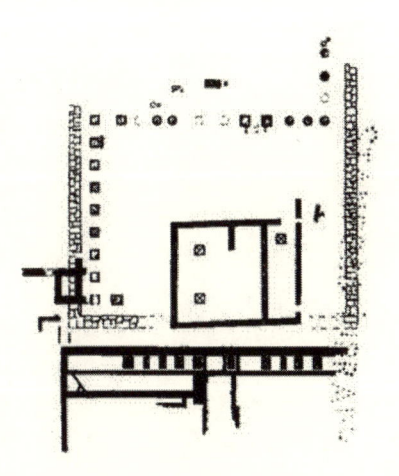

1:600   THEBES.   CHAPEL OF QUEEN AND TEMPLE OF AMENHOTEP II.   XXIII.

■ BRICK,   ▩ BRICK XXIII DYN.,   ▨ STONE BASES,   ▦ STONE FOUNDATIONS.

1:600 THEBES. TEMPLE OF TAHUTMES IV.

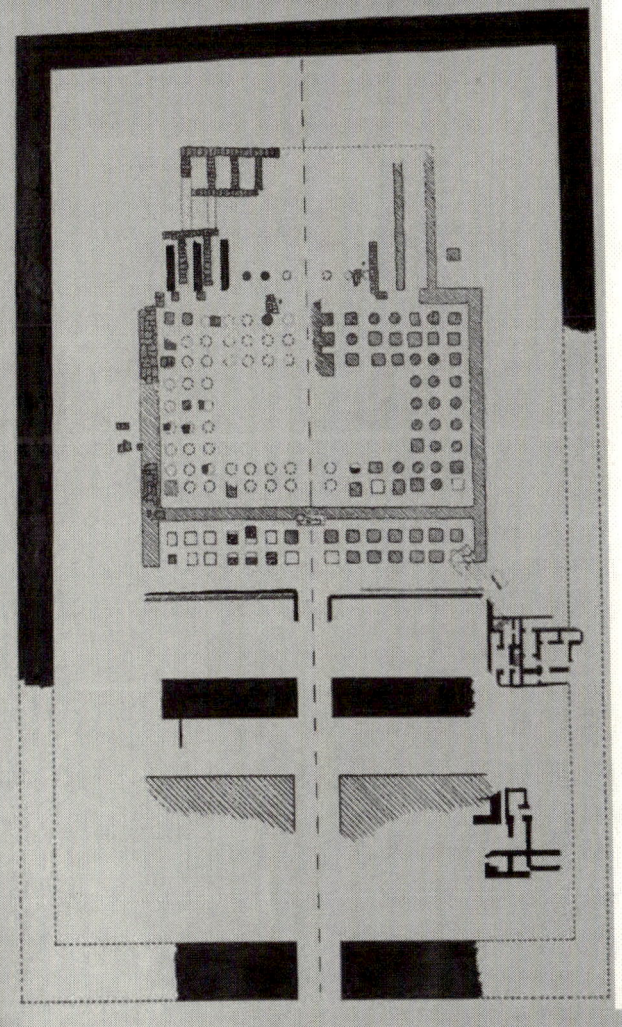

■ BRICK, ▧ PAVEMENT, ▨ STONE FOUNDATION, ▨ FOUNDATION HOLLOWS.

1:600　　　THEBES. TEMPLE OF MERENPTAH.　　　XXV.

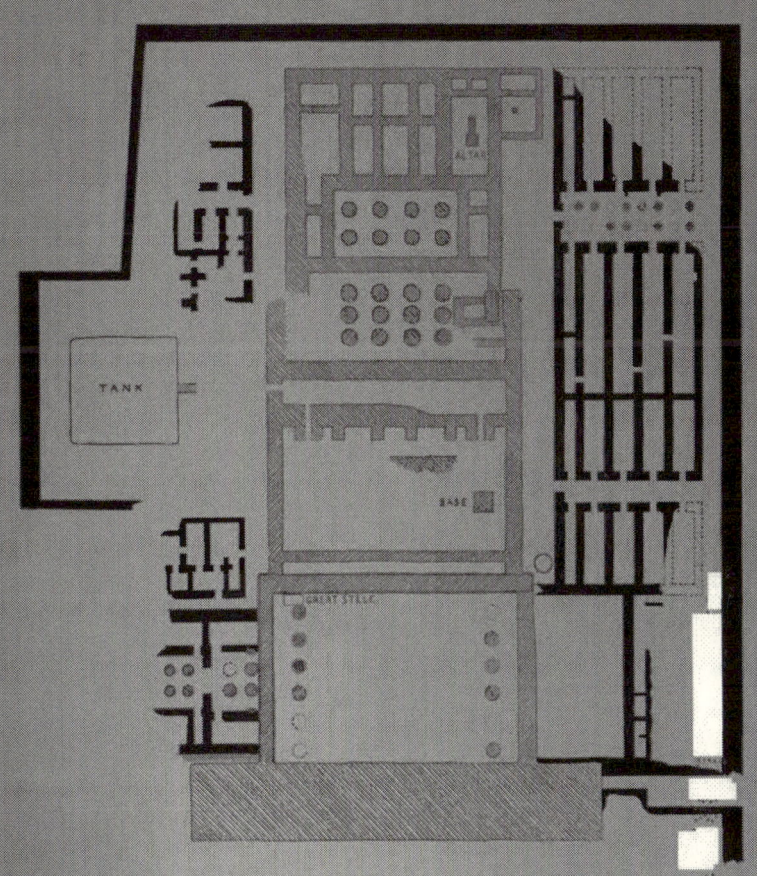

■ BRICK,　　STONE FOUNDATION　　FOUNDATION HOLLOWS

THEBES. TEMPLES AND CHAPELS. XXVI.

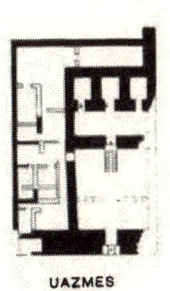

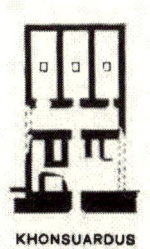

1:600

UAZMES

KHONSUARDUS

SIPTAH

TAUSERT

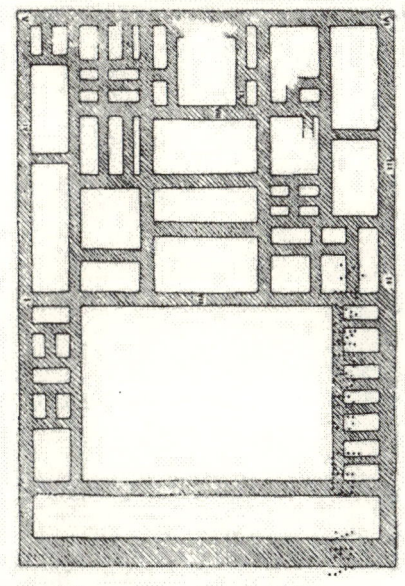

■ BRICK   ~~~ FOUNDATION HOLLOWS   I to IX DEPOSITS

Made in the USA
Middletown, DE
15 March 2024